A Deepening Love Affair

A DEEPENING LOVE AFFAIR

The Gift of God in Later Life

JANE MARIE THIBAULT

UPPER
ROOM BOOKS
NASHVILLE

A DEEPENING LOVE AFFAIR
The Gift of God in Later Life

The Upper Room Web Site: http://www.upperroom.org

Cover design: Bruce Gore/Gore Studio
Cover photograph: Chris Alan Wilton/The Image Bank
First printing: November 1993; Second printing: October 1994
Third printing: March 1995; Fourth printing: January 1998
ISBN: 0-8358-0685-5
Library of Congress Catalog Card Number: 93-60483

Printed in the United States of America on acid-free paper

With deep gratitude
and still-growing love,
this book is dedicated
to the memoried presence of

THE REVEREND STANISLAUS J. GOYETTE

A French-Canadian parish priest,
Curé de Saint Louis de France,
he came unannounced into my life
—bearing gifts—
in the week of the Perseids
the year I was 9.

Gentling the storms of
a frightened family,
he quickened our lives
—then died—just 56,
in the season of Pentecost
the year I was 12.

He was the Christ-gift
to my childhood,
taking hand-in-hand with me
that first—
tiny—
terrified—
ecstatic!
baby-step
into the Kingdom of God.

CONTENTS

ACKNOWLEDGMENTS

MORE PEOPLE THAN I COULD POSSIBLY NAME AND THANK have enabled me to write this book. Much inspiration, encouragement, and many sources of reflection have come from the two faith communities that are dear to my heart and to which I belong— Beechmont United Methodist Church and Saint John Vianney *caution* Catholic Church, both of which "live" within a few blocks of one another in the south end of Louisville, Kentucky. This "double belonging," dual interfaith relationship has been an incredibly challenging and rich source of spiritual growth and development for me. I know that without the love, support, nurture, and encouragement of the people of these relatively small Christian communities, this book would not have been conceived, nor would it have come to birth. It is primarily with these people in mind—all members of the ultimate community of the Trinity, the kingdom of God—and *for* them, that I have written.

A number of folks I want to thank specifically. They are:

All of those people who are mentioned by name in the text of the book, who generously provided the "stories" which give life to the theory.

Rev. Paul Shepherd, former pastor of Beechmont United Methodist Church, whose initial idea it was for me to write this book and who "called" me to do it by phoning Janice Grana at The Upper Room and warning her that he had a gerontologist involved in spirituality on the loose in his congregation and could she do something about it?

Father J. Roy Stiles, my friend and mentor, and pastor of St. John Vianney parish, who carefully read (and reread, ad infinitum) and critiqued each draft of this book. His own long-term interest in the well-being of older adults and his belief in the value of this project, as well as his excellent yet very kind and gentle suggestions for revision, were a constant source of support and encouragement. His willingness to walk through this with me kept me from giving up on this labor countless times—right up to the day this book-child was due!

My chairman, Dr. Kenneth Holtzapple, and colleagues in the Department of Family and Community Medicine of the University of Louisville School of Medicine, who showed continued interest with frequent "How's the book coming along?" and were patient enough to listen to my complaints.

All my friends whom I have neglected for the past year, who have graciously (with a few exceptions) put up with my neglect without complaint.

To my parents, Dewey J. Thibault and Jeannette E. Deschenes, I give praise and thanksgiving for the gift of my life and for the values they lived and bequeathed—their spiritual legacy, which lives on in my heart. I also feel a deep need to express some form of appreciation to the Jewish congregation of Temple Beth El in Fall River, Massachusetts. This is the community that awakened me to the reality of God, through my friend Barbara Zukroff and her family. Because of our childhood friendship, Temple Beth El also became *my* synagogue, my "baby temple," as I call it now. My father and I drove by it every morning on the way to school from kindergarten to the third grade. As we sat at the stop sign, I would read—each day without exception—the inscription over the doors: "Seek God While He May Be Found." This quotation from Isaiah has remained the primary quest of my life.

I thank the people from my earlier years who, after the deaths of my parents voluntarily and spontaneously housed, fed, and clothed me, mothered and fathered me, brothered and sistered me, mentored me, and gave me new life. They are Cecile, George, Judy, Don, and Chris McNamara; Marjorie, Leo, Peter, and Bonnie Strickman; Marian, David, Linda, and Jeff Greer; Helen Thumm Grossman and Ade Bethune. And a few years later, the Vonder Haar family. All of these people, who rest gently in my heart, continue to nourish my life.

Rev. Adrien Bernier and Rev. Adrian J. Cooney, OCD, now both deceased, took my spiritual interests seriously and nurtured my teenage desire for a life of prayer. It was through the counsel of Rev. Cooney that I experienced the "call" to work with older adults and the "push" to study for my doctorate in aging.

My wonderful family are among the most joyous of the gifts I have been given in my lifetime. Mother-in-law Frances Krieg and Bethany Joy Fryrear (who is both stepdaughter and goddaughter) provide me with much laughter, love, and the stability and security of real family life.

Ronald Fryrear, my husband, is a special gift of the Spirit to my life. Without my groundedness in his love and the daily life we create together, I would probably not be able to do this work. I tend to get overwhelmed easily and threaten to give it all up fairly often. At these times, Ron never fails to come through with some kind of creative response to allay my fears. When I was discouraged and thinking about abandoning my Ph.D. dissertation, very close to its completion, he said nothing but went to the music stand, took up his trombone, and played a blaring rendition of "Pomp and Circumstance," wordlessly encouraging me to imagine myself walking down the aisle on graduation day. When I complained that I did not want, nor did I have time to do research on a restraint-free chair two colleagues and I had designed and patented, he looked up from his dinner plate and said, "Do you want to be tied up when you are older?" No. "Do you want old people to be tied up now?" No. "Then, you know what you have to do." Point made.

My fearful and frustrated ranting and raving occurs with such regularity that Ron has recently developed a litany which he recites to me and has me repeat. It eliminates the need for him to be so creative. That litany is:

Keep your mind on what you are doing;
Remember why you are doing it;
Remember who you are doing it for
and you'll be just fine!

And when things get *really* bad, he takes me fishing!

A multitude of thanks are also due to Janice Grana, Lynne Deming, and Robin Pippin, my editors at The Upper Room—and also to John Mogabgab, editor of *Weavings,* in which the story of Catherine first appeared. Lynne reminded me recently that this book will have taken seven years from conception to its birth. What a gestation period! In all that time, as I kept procrastinating yet reaffirming the fact that I truly did desire to write, there were words of encouragement only. I am deeply grateful for their faith in me; these are truly people who live what they publish. Involvement with them, through the writing of this book, has been an incredible source of spiritual nourishment.

At the risk of being trite, I want to acknowledge my appreciation of two fur-persons, tiny creatures who kept me company during the early morning hours of this endeavor. The cats Sheba and Spike showed up, uninvited, on our back doorstep a couple of years ago at Christmastime, and adopted us, dog and all. We were not cat-lovers, but they obviously needed a home and we needed to rid ourselves of mice. So they stayed. And they have become spiritual companions in their own little ways. As I finish this book I cannot remember one morning during the past nine months when both haven't roused themselves from sleep to cuddle around the computer while I wrote, every once in a while stretching out a paw that touched my hand. Their company allayed my anxiety and comforted me in a way that enabled me to center and be receptive to the thoughts that needed to be written. They "pitched their tents" beside me and all was well; God's love is so delightfully manifested in all manner of great and tiny things!

INTRODUCTION

A FEW YEARS AGO CATHERINE H., AN AFFLUENT SIXTY-SEVEN-year-old widow of a local surgeon, came to talk to me. She complained that something was not quite right with her life but, try as she might, she had not been able to determine what was wrong.

During our conversation Catherine spoke of her involvement in all of the benefits we associate with retirement—travel, club functions, volunteer activities and church work, close friendships, control over her own time, and grandchildren who actually sought her company! In addition, she was enjoying very good health. As she spoke of her travels around the world and her adventures as an antique importer, I thought to myself, not a little enviously, "What a lovely life this lady has. If she's not happy with all of this meaningful activity, she must be clinically depressed!" I proceeded to mentally race ahead of her story so that I could come up with a fitting diagnosis and a plan for treatment.

One phrase stopped my thoughts dead in their tracks. She said, in a tone close to desperation, "I am playing antique bingo in the same way that other, less fortunate people play real bingo—just to kill time amusing myself." She claimed that despite her family, friends, work, travel, lovely home, and wealth, she was missing something. I suggested that she might still be grieving the loss of her husband. She laughed and said, "Honey, he died twenty years ago. We had a lovely life, and I was sad for a few years; but I pulled myself together, and I've certainly enjoyed my life since then! No, what I'm feeling now is not grief."

She went back to the antique bingo theme, suddenly caught up in the thoughts she was expressing. "You know, I've kept very busy all of my life. I've always had something to do, somewhere to go, somebody to be with. And now I don't want to do any of that; I don't savor anything! I used to be active in many things but lately I find myself withdrawing from many of my activities, so much so that friends and family are becoming worried about me. To be honest, my daughter is the one who insisted on my coming to see you! She thinks I'm depressed, but I don't really think I am, because underneath it all I have this feeling that there's more to life than what I have experienced. I don't know what that is, but I crave it and nothing else satisfies me. I think my problem is that I just can't get in touch with what this 'something more' is. I am so frustrated!"

I realized at that moment that this lively woman was not depressed in the ordinary, clinical sense. Instead, what she seemed to be experiencing was a loss of the sense of meaning in her life. As we continued to talk, I learned that she was fairly content with the value of her daily activities to her own and others' well-being. However, she did not have a strong sense of the ultimate meaning and purpose of her life. Life was pleasant, but no longer intense, and often she found herself bored. The more she tried to distract herself by work or play, the more discontented she became.

I asked her about her spiritual life. "I go to church every Sunday morning and Wednesday evening. I have taught Sunday School for the past twenty-six years and have been president of one church committee or another for my entire adult life," she replied, "but church doesn't help, either. I'm bored with my church, my friends, my minister, the Bible. I think I'm even bored with God. I don't get too excited about the problem of salvation. I think I've lived a fairly Christian life, and I don't fear death. Church—religion—just doesn't seem to speak to the way I feel. It's just another activity, and I'm even pulling away from that."

"That's your church life," I said. "What is going on between you and God?" There was a long pause.

"Nothing," she replied, "and to be perfectly honest, there are times in the middle of some nights, when I wonder whether there really is a God, or at least a God who is concerned about the minutiae of human life! Sometimes I wonder if religion is an arbitrary story to explain and organize life. Yet there are other times when I crave God, but can't make the connection." She paused, then her eyes widened, as though she had just discovered something. "I know what it is I want—and nothing else will do: I want to experience God. I want to know who—what—if God is. I want to sink into God and let myself go! It seems as though I've been behaving well and working for someone I've read and heard about, but have never met, Well, it's high time we met!" Her next question was "Where do I go from here?"

"Where do I go from here?" is the question I address in this book. It is the primary research question I have asked in my sixteen years as a gerontologist and the one I have pursued personally since the age of eighteen.

My Journey of the Spirit

Let me share with you a bit about myself. During my mid-teen years both of my parents died, thirteen months apart, after suffering long and lingering illnesses. For two years after their deaths I experienced a deep depression that seemed more than normal grief. I was left with an intense sense of the meaninglessness of daily living and was incapable of enjoying anything. Normal adolescent activities held no interest; school was a chore, but my only escape. Church attendance didn't help.

Aware that all was not well with my mind and soul, I asked to see a psychiatrist, but was told that I was doing fine and did not need to see one. There was little understanding of the stages of grief in the early 1960's, and I did not allow myself to appear depressed, so as not to jeopardize my living situation. It was not readily apparent to others that I was in deep pain. I looked around in books for answers to my extremely negative (at times suicidal) state of mind. I read popular and academic texts in psychology, psychiatry, sociology, philosophy, and theology, but nothing hit the mark; nothing explained the emptiness, the lack of meaning I felt in my life.

One day, while browsing in a college bookstore, I came across a small paperback book entitled *Seeds of Contemplation* by a Trappist monk from Kentucky named Thomas Merton. I took it home and in its pages found what I had been seeking for so long, but didn't know it—a statement that God dwells within each of us, that God is able to be known by experience, and that God actually craves an intimate relationship with all of God's children. Merton went on to say that the primary purpose of life is to become increasingly aware of the presence of the Father, Son, and Spirit in the soul and of one's relationship with them. In a flash I knew two things—that this union with God was the one thing I wanted for my own life and it was also what I wanted to contribute to life by helping other people become aware of their own invitation to such a relationship. I was certain that without this mutual encounter with God my life would continue to be meaningless. The question then became, as it did for Catherine, "Where do I go from here?" With that question, my conscious spiritual journey began.

My journey in and of the Spirit is now in its thirtieth year. It has been a great adventure, and as I advance in age it becomes an even more amazing gift to me. It has taken me through centuries of spiritual literature and sacred places. It has put me in contact with current masters of the spiritual life. It has enriched my knowledge and provided my education. It has gifted me with my husband and family, and with loving guides and mentors and friends and colleagues who share the same desire for God. It has become the source of my life's work. Most of all, it has led me into a love affair that deepens and intensifies as the years go by. The attempt to be in an ever-more-intense relationship with a God who loves me and is concerned about me as an individual as well as a member of the human community has given my life the joy and meaning that nothing else could possibly have provided. This does not mean that I have not doubted, that I have not felt greatly abandoned at times, that I have not been angry with God and that I have not wanted and tried to abandon the journey—to "harden my heart."

But the call to this relationship is irresistible.

While in college, I majored in English and psychology and became interested in psychological growth and development throughout the life span. It appeared that there was a great deal of information about early life and young adulthood, but that most of the knowledge stopped at middle age. I became fascinated with the idea of wisdom and thought that if wisdom were to be found at any stage of the life cycle, it would most likely be in the later years. I decided to study gerontology—the science of aging.

My professional work in the medical setting has focused on the physiological, psychological, and sociological aspects of the aging process. As the director of a geriatric evaluation and treatment unit at the University of Louisville School of Medicine, I encounter elderly patients and their families on a daily basis. I teach classes to medical students and family medicine residents. My research is varied, but most of it focuses on the spiritual experience of older adults and the church's response to the spiritual needs of the mature adult. Since my meeting with Catherine, I have interviewed a large number of older adults who have discussed with me their own spiritual journeys.

A Deepening Love Affair

Of one thing I am convinced—our mainline Protestant and Catholic churches do not respond as well as they might to the hunger for spiritual experience that often emerges in the mature Christian. Our Western culture is embarrassed by emotion. Because we take such great pride in our rationality, we are afraid of such encounters as John Wesley described in his Aldersgate experience, when he felt his heart "strangely warmed." Yet loving faith is not just an intellectual assent to written truths. Faith is a total response of body, intellect, and emotions to a truth about the universe and our lives in it that is personal and immediate, as well as impersonal and transcendent. What we often do not realize is that the response is reciprocal—God, the object of our faith, hope, and love, seeks us first and wants to relate to us in a personal, intimate way. God has designed us to be able to realize with our whole being—body, mind, and soul—that we are involved in a truly cosmic love affair.

I believe that all too often our church life does little to awaken us to the knowledge that our relationship with God can be and should be a true love affair with God. The church seems to be embarrassed by such an intensity of relationship. It focuses on Christian ethical behavior and the salvation of souls—all very important, to be sure. But this is not enough to satisfy some souls, souls who want to fall into the arms of God in a love that is all-consuming. Perhaps not many of us really want to be totally consumed by the love of God. It appears easier to keep God at a distance so that we may control the course of our lives. But when we insist on always being in control, we lose some of the abundance of life, the vital part of the gift for which we were made.

Problems of Language

We talk much in this book about this "deepening love affair," of falling in love and being in love with God. Some people I have spoken with are disturbed by the use of such language in discussing the soul's relationship with God. It sounds too sensual, even sexual, and alien to what one's relationship with God "ought" to be. These individuals want a more intense relationship with God, but they are uncomfortable with the language that describes the experience of love they are called to. One woman said to me "I don't like all this 'God is my boyfriend' stuff." So she rejects the invitation to a deeper relationship because she is put off by the sexual overtones.

Yet this is not a sexual relationship, even though the language used may sound that way. The reason for the use of sexual imagery throughout the ages is that we have no language of the spirit, no words to describe the total intimacy and otherness of God. For example, we use *He*—or try something genderless that doesn't work very well. God is not even person in the sense that we mean it when we speak of human beings. But we do need to work God and our relationship with God into our language in some way, and we do the best we can with the language closest to what describes our experience. How does one describe an intensifying relationship with God in the language of our times?

The Primary Spiritual Task of Later Life

I have come to believe that the development of an intense, mutual, love relationship with God is the primary spiritual task of later life. I have encountered some older adults who have made this discovery and who seem to be growing more vital and more loving every day. I have met others, also churchgoers, sometimes the pillars of the church, who are jaded, bitter, bored by it all. They "do their thing" at church, but the inner spirit has stagnated.

Finally, I've encountered many, many others who are spiritually discontented but do not know why. They would like to go beyond their state of discontent, but they do not know how to do so. They do not even know what is wrong with them. Some believe they are losing their faith and feel guilty and worried. Others leave their churches to seek new experiences in other congregations or denominations, thinking that perhaps the messages of a new pastor might help. Rarely do they confide their spiritual longings to anyone, as Catherine did to me—perhaps because no one has ever asked them about their own spiritual journey. Rarely do they get beyond their discontent. Due to lack of new vision and encouragement, they resign themselves to a kind of spiritual apathy.

I have written this book for the mature adult who is spiritually discontented. The state of being spiritually discontented is an extremely significant state of being. It can lead either to a radical deepening of faith or to a virtual abandonment of living faith. The difficulty is that the answer, the cure for this state of soul, lies within. Discontent cannot be assuaged from without: by doing more good works, heading more committees, joining the choir. Many mature Christians have spent entire lifetimes serving Christ, following the precepts of the social gospel, diligently studying scripture, doing faithfully what they were called to do as servants of their Lord. When this no longer gives satisfaction, they add new external activities, to no avail. Some are too tired, too "burned out" to try new activities, and they sink back into a belief that "this is all there is—I may as well be contented with it. I'll wait for more after death."

How do we move beyond this painful place? I believe that inner work is the next step. Inner work takes us from an outwardly fruitful, mature Christian life to the fulfillment of faith. It takes us straight to the heart of God. In some ways inner work is much more difficult than external work, especially for those of us living in the second half of the twentieth century. Our society (which includes our churches) does not seem to value inner work because its products are not readily visible. However, it is the inner work that transforms, so that we can come to say, as did Paul, "It is no longer I who live, but it is Christ who lives in me" (Gal. 2:20 NRSV).

This book deals with the inner work that I consider to be the spiritual life task of the mature adult. There is nothing new in these pages except my unwavering conviction that those who are privileged to be experiencing late life have the challenge and opportunity to embark on a new vocation. That vocation is the call, the invitation to experience the union of an ever-deepening love affair with God in this life. I am convinced that God has saved the best for last.

1

❦

THE RADICAL FREEDOM OF AGE

We know that by turning everything to their good God co-operates with all those who love him, with all those that he has called according to his purpose. They are the ones he chose specially long ago and intended to become true images of his Son, so that his Son might be the eldest of many brothers. He called those he intended for this; those he called he justified, and with those he justified he shared his glory.

Romans 8:28-30

WHY HAVE YOU AND THOUSANDS OF OTHER OLDER ADULTS BEEN gifted with so many years at this particular time in history?

Think seriously about it. This generation of people sixty-five and older is the first generation in the history of humankind to have been given such a long life span. This does not mean that there were not people who lived to a ripe old age in the past. There were, but they were few and far between; they were oddities; and because they were so few they did not pose the same challenges to society that your generation does. You are a dangerous generation.

If you were born in 1900, your average life expectancy was forty-seven. If you are living to read this, then, obviously, you and many others were gifted far beyond expectation. There are more one-hundred-year-old people in the world today than there ever have been. Ponder this again and again: You are the first generation in the history of humankind to live this long. Why you?

Perhaps there is no reason floating out in there in the universe to be captured. Perhaps a reason must be created out of the inner spirit of love, then given as Eucharist to each other, accepted, and stewarded. What if the reason is that your generation is being asked to show the world how to come back to its spirit? What if the reason is that you must, with all of your remaining strength, attempt to demonstrate to the world how to live and how to love one another as Christ loves us? What if the reason for your abundant years is that as many of you as possible must become Christ-gift to the world?

Not "Dry Bones"

Some of you have bought into the myth that you are "dry bones" and good for nothing but bingo. You have a vocation that can bring you and all the rest of us into the kingdom here and now. Yet you say that you are too old, that your bones are too dry, that it is too late, that you want to rest and be left to rest.

But God said to Ezekiel:

"Son of man, these bones are the whole House of Israel. They keep saying, 'Our bones are dried up, our hope has gone; we are as good as dead'. So, prophesy. Say to them, 'The Lord Yahweh says this: I am now going to open your graves; I mean to raise you from your graves, my people. And I shall put my spirit in you, and you will live, and I shall resettle you on your own soil; and you will know that I, Yahweh, have said and done this—it is the Lord Yahweh who speaks.' "

Ezekiel 37:11-14

What is this "opening of your grave" that comes in the later years, in the winter of the life span? What is the soil on which God promises to resettle you? What can dry, old, painful, brittle, tired, osteoporotic bones do now that they could not do earlier in life, or better yet, that some younger person could not do now? Why would God be calling an *old person*?

God is calling you, an old person, out of your grave. You are well prepared for your own, personal resurrection because in addition to the gift of God's presence, you and your peers alone have been given radical freedom. The *radical freedom of age*. You are what the scientists call a "critical mass," a group of people who exist in large enough numbers to make a difference in the world because more than the energy of one person is needed for this work. (Just as an example, the AARP—American Association of Retired Persons—is the second largest and most powerful lobby group in the United States, second only to the National Rifle Association.)

More so than ever before or will probably ever be again in the near future, older adults have the freedom that retirement brings. It is the freedom of time, place, mobility, relative wellness, energy, and, for a great many, adequate finances. For the most part, you are free to do what you want to do when you want to do it, in the manner in which you want to do it. Even in the nursing home, which may be perceived to be captivity, there is relative freedom to spend hours and hours as you want to, thinking your own thoughts or being involved with others as it suits you. And especially if you live in your own home, there is the tremendous freedom of time. How are you to respond to this gift of time, this radical freedom that retirement brings?

Be assured that whoever you are, however old you are, wherever you are, above all other things God who is Abba is calling you to a life of intimate, loving relationship. God wants you to know and feel how very, very much you are loved and wanted, cherished and gifted—and needed. Needed by God and by the whole body of Christ. God wants and delights in continuing to gift you with all that is God's self. God wants to join in creative partnership with you to gift the rest of the world. All you need to do is ask for awareness of your gifts, accept them with gratefulness, and nurture them as good stewards. Then when it is time, return them—with the gift of your own self—to God, in one, final, flaming gift of love for the well-being of all of creation.

I invite you in the next chapter to consider your life as gift. The willingness to allow yourself to look at later life differently, to become aware of the reality of the gifts that are constantly being offered you could become the gateway to a radically new stage in your life, a new way of being—for yourself and for countless others of your own generation and of generations to come.

2

❦

GIFTEDNESS:
A SPIRITUALITY FOR THE LATER YEARS

Bless Yahweh, my soul,
bless his holy name, all that is in me!
Bless Yahweh, my soul,
and remember all his kindnesses.

Psalm 103:1-2

ALL THAT IS, IS GIFT: GOD-GIFT. All people. All places. All things. Gift of the Creator to the created. Of the Father to his children. Of the Son to his friends. Of the Lover to the beloved. Of the Mother to us all. Of all of us to one another.

I began thinking about the concept of "gift" as a way of looking at life and as an attitude toward life particularly suited to the later years after I survived a collision with an eighteen-wheel truck while driving on Interstate 64 on October 2, 1990. After crawling headfirst out of the passenger-side window of my battered car, which had finally come to a halt at the trunk of an old sycamore tree, I wobbled around in a field in a daze for a few minutes before people were able to come to me.

What I remember most was being totally aware of nothing but the intense greenness of the grass, the blueness of the sky, a few puffs of cloud overhead, and some birds squawking raucously in the tree. I was alive to experience this! What blessing, what *gift* everything was in that one moment!

After the accident I began to challenge myself to look for the "giftness" in everything, on a minute-by-minute basis.

Interestingly, from 1987 until the time of the accident I had been unable to begin writing this book. Try as I might, I could find no central, coordinating theme around which to talk about the relationship we are invited to enjoy with God in later life. *Gift* quickly became that theme. Was the accident a gift? No, it wasn't; but my ability to translate it into a theme for my life and for this book certainly was—I could not have come to the realization of total giftedness out of my own limited creativity.

Before you read any further, please relax, take a deep breath (the gift of oxygen), and consider for a moment the idea of gift and its connection to your life. Do you agree with my initial statement that all that is, is gift? If yes, why? If no, why not? Do you feel that you have been receiving gifts since your conception? Are you aware of the gifts you have received over the course of your lifetime?

If you find the idea of gift true to your experience, are you able to live your life in an ever-growing awareness of the gifts you are given, minute by minute, day by day, year by year? Do you realize also that you are a gift and a source of new gifts to others? Do you recognize the way in which the gifts you have received and the gifts you have given have shaped your very life? Perhaps you haven't given gifts much thought. Let's explore this idea together, starting with an attempt to define the word *gift*.

Just What Is a Gift?

Webster defines the word *gift* very briefly as "anything given." That's all. This simple definition implies that there is a receiver, but Webster doesn't speak of the characteristics of the one who receives the gift. The emphasis appears to be on the act of giving. Then what does *give* mean? To give is a complex, active process having a variety of meanings. In its most common usage and understanding, *to give* means to bestow freely, without a return. But to give also means to accord as a trust, to commit to another, to serve, to announce, to produce, to offer to the action of another, to present for consideration, to open or give way, and, lastly, to afford a view or passage. God engages in all of these activities in giving us gifts.

As the product of the act of giving, *gift* also has many meanings. One important characteristic of a gift is that, very often, it is wrapped up in paper and ribbon or enclosed in some kind of covering that hides it from the view of the receiver. The person who is given the gift is the only one who has the right as well as the responsibility of unwrapping the gift. Sometimes gifts are so well-wrapped that it takes some effort to undo the paper and ribbon. Sometimes we need help from others to unwrap our gift.

The feeling that we have when we are in the process of unwrapping our gift is usually one of delighted expectancy. We pay attention to it and focus most of our attention on it. We try to guess what is inside. We have a combined feeling of not being worthy mixed with the feeling of being special. We usually say to the giver something like "Oh, you shouldn't have done this!" (But we don't really mean it.) We are excited, exalted out of our usual humdrumness. We try to imagine what might be inside. We feel happy.

Most of all, we feel connected to the giver, who also waits in hushed expectancy to see if we will appreciate what has been given, the effort that has been made to find the perfect gift to match the need or the taste of the one receiving. There is a certain communion of being. Something takes place in the moment between the giving of the gift and its final unwrapping that is very special, full of promise and uniting the giver with the one who receives, in a relationship that transcends the gift itself.

Have you ever tried to shortchange your family by deciding *not* to wrap their Christmas presents? A few years ago I decided that it would be much more efficient and practical to put our family's Christmas presents in nicely colored boxes and dispense with the cost, time, and effort we usually expend on wrapping and tying. I was very pleased with myself and thought that Ron and Bethany would be pleased also. Not so! They both protested vehemently, saying that they enjoyed the whole ritual of wrapping and unwrapping. In great detail they told me how much they like to choose the right kind of paper, how they challenge themselves to cut it into the most economic size, and how much they enjoy being creative with ribbon in the final decoration of the box. Most of all, they enjoy the look of pleasure on the face of the person presented with such a box. They let me know in no uncertain terms that they liked receiving such gifts, and, needless to say, I never made that suggestion again!

Perhaps, summarizing all of the above, we can say that a gift is something given to another for the increased well-being and happiness of that person. Also implied is that the giver somehow benefits from the process and act of giving. Could God ever benefit from our receiving the gifts we are given? If so, how could this be?

Gifted throughout Life

What gifts are you aware of having received—from other people? from God?

When I ask this question of individuals or groups of people, most hesitate and admit that they don't think they have been given very many gifts. This attitude suggests that they are thinking of gifts as something extraordinary, something beyond the simple everydayness of life—the "big" gifts. Usually they think I am referring to gifts of the Spirit or special talents. We will talk about "special" gifts later in the book. Here I am referring to the tremendous bounty of gifts we have received every day of our lives since the moment of conception. Do you ever ponder the fact that your very life and all that exists around you, that which is right beyond your nose to the matter floating in the outer boundaries of the known universe, is a gift to you from the Creator?

We are not accustomed to thinking about our existence in this way. Twentieth-century American culture teaches us very effectively from an early age to think of ourselves as the *doers*, not the receivers—active, independent, productive beings—who think of ourselves as the cause of our own activity, our own well-being.

Yet, when we examine this view closely, we find that it doesn't "fit" with reality.

The Gifts of Your Life

What is the reality, then? Take a look at your life, starting from the very beginning, in search of your basic gifts. First of all, are you the cause of your own existence? Of course not. You are here because in their union your parents were gifts to each other (whether or not they fully realized it or intended to be). Then, by a gift of God, the potential for fully mature human life was breathed into you at the moment of your conception. Immediately after conception, your mother provided you with the gift of her hospitality, which you enjoyed for forty weeks (give or take a few). In that warm, secure womb you grew from one cell to billions of cells. You were nourished by her food, her oxygen, her already-established blood supply, her emotions. You were lulled by her heartbeat, soothed or aroused by her voice. You played in the pool of her amniotic fluid and even enjoyed sucking the gift of your own thumb! At your birth you were washed and welcomed by others eager to meet you—father, family, friends, or even professionals on site to assist.

After birth you were fed with milk from your mother—or from a cow, which donated to your cause. Then came food, grown and made available to you as gifts from farmers unknown and unseen. You played with toys created and presented to you by others. You received the gift of touch, were cuddled physically and emotionally by those who held you. This was not a luxury, for your central nervous system needed this touch in order for your brain to develop and to enable you to survive.

You were provided with the gift of a sheltering home. If you lived in an urban area you probably enjoyed the benefits of public facilities such as water and electricity and the products of business. Did the milkman, the ice man, the egg man, and the bread man come to your door? If you lived in a rural area, you had the chance to see where water came from, how light and bread were actually made, how animals came into being and became food for you.

You were taught language, a major gift; for with the understanding of words and the ability to use them began the process of developing your sense of self and your independence. From that point on the newly-learned, highly complex skill of naming and knowing the purpose and meaning of objects you saw in the outer world and sensations you felt within your body provided you with your own means of gifting yourself with knowledge and awareness of everything around you. The gift of words created a bridge that put you in relationship with all of creation through your understanding of those things that existed outside of yourself.

At around the age of five or so you were given the opportunity to go to school, an incredibly complex and expensive social institution. The people (known and unknown) of your larger community who cared for your well-being and potential were willing to sacrifice time and money to provide you with an education. Whether or not you were able to take advantage of this gift, it was available to you for twelve years. You may have had the opportunity to receive a college or even a graduate level of education, depending on the circumstances of your life. At school you learned not only facts and information, but skills that would enable you to enter society as an independent person, able to take care of yourself and others, able to make a living, able to create a home, able to contribute gifts to society.

In addition to an education, your parents and other adults in the religious community may have provided you with an opportunity to learn the story of the creation of the universe and to experience the gift of God's love of you as an individual and of the whole world. You were thus given your heritage—your true place as a member of the family of God.

As you grew and matured, your peers became gift to you, challenging your interpersonal skills and talents, urging you to go beyond your immediate family in your loyalty and ability to find pleasure and satisfaction. Through them, you learned to experience empathy, the ability to imagine how another person might be thinking or feeling. This would be the key to the ongoing growth of your ability to relate to other human beings.

After school you may have experienced the gift of a loving relationship with another. You may have found the person whom you loved with a love that went beyond the desire to fulfill your own needs. This person may have become your mate. While you may have actively searched for him or her, you could not coerce that person into becoming your spouse—he or she gave the gift of self to you. The development of your love relationship was a mutual gift of your bodies, minds, and souls to each other.

In addition to a spouse, you might have been blessed with the gift of children, your own or the children of others who looked up to you as a special friend. The gift of a relationship with a child provides you with a way to guide and influence the future of world, from generation to generation. It also keeps you in touch with and nurtures the little child who still lives within you.

Marriage or the life of a single person brought with it the responsibilities of early adulthood. At this time you searched for and may have been gifted with the kind of work you wanted to spend your time doing. Perhaps you felt called in some way to a particular work for God and/or for other human beings. Not all of us have the opportunity to take advantage of this gift of enjoyable or committed work; some of us must endure boring, backbreaking labor in order to make a living. It is when the work is unendurable that we realize that satisfying, fulfilling work is a true gift.

As you have matured, the gifts of the natural environment may have become a source of deep peace and great joy for you. You may find yourself feeling an increasing sense of connection with and love of basic, elemental things like wild animals, trees, earth, water, rocks, and sky. You might be enjoying the changes and variety of weather in a way you never did before. Thunderstorms may arouse in you a newfound sense of awe. You may be yearning to spend more and more time alone, enjoying the gifts of nature. With this appreciation, you may experience a deepening sense of personal responsibility for the well-being of these earth-things.

At some point in life you might have become truly aware of the gift of your body. I say *truly* because, while we all experience our bodies, some of us go through life never fully appreciating the physical self with its incredible workings, amazing strength, and potential for pleasure. Most of us don't realize that in nearly every organ system, we have been gifted with far more cells than we actually need to see us through a good, long lifetime. We may never have experienced the awe of the realization that we are "fearfully and wonderfully made" (Psalm 139:14 NRSV). Many of us are afraid of our senses of touch, taste, smell, hearing, and sight. We "use" them for the necessary work of life, but fail to appreciate the pleasure they afford us and the ways in which they connect us to one another and all of creation.

Perhaps you came to appreciate your body at an early age, when you first felt the warmth of sand between your toes, a baseball plop perfectly into your glove, a race exhaustingly well-run. Or perhaps when you were older and your entire body responded so completely and wonderfully to your love of another person. Perhaps you had never thought of your body as gift until it was gift to another, during pregnancy or childbirth. Perhaps you did not appreciate the gift of your body until its health was gone or you experienced a time of intense pain or chronic suffering. Perhaps, because of early childhood abuse of one kind or another, your body has never been your own, to know and to experience and to use.

It is at the time of ill health or pain that the gift of the body is sometimes most appreciated. Have you had a major, life-threatening illness? Are you in chronic pain? Have you experienced the gift that modern medicine can be to cure you or to keep you functioning independently? Does medicine keep your pain from interfering with the way you want to live your life? If so, despite its cost and inconvenience, the art and science of modern medicine is true gift to you.

Perhaps one of the greatest of all gifts is the ability to think, to know, to understand—the gift of the mind. For most of your life you have probably taken your mind for granted, unless you have experienced from childhood some particular difficulty in learning, which made you acutely aware that your mind wasn't working in quite the same way as everyone else's. You probably didn't give the gift of your mind much thought until you first started experiencing the normal changes in memory functioning that come with age. It is at this point, somewhere in mid-age, that you might have noticed the first signs that your mind does not seem to work as quickly or as efficiently as previously. Your mind was then forced to think about itself, something that only human beings are capable of doing! And in the thinking about itself, it comes to appreciate the tremendous gift that it truly is. This gift of the mind is what connects us to all that exists, and it allows us to be in intimate relationship with others. It connects our present with past and future. It enables us to grow, to stretch and expand our awareness. It enables us to transcend our small and often petty selves. It is the vehicle by which we can begin to know God.

The gifts I have just mentioned are the most obvious ones, the ones that are basic to the experience of most people in this culture and in this time. You may have been given these gifts to greater or lesser degrees and in ways different from the experience of other people, but you have received at least the basic ones. As magnificent and awesome as these basic gifts are, they are commonly overlooked or taken for granted, primarily because they are to be found in everyday existence. What we see every day we very often fail to see. How often do we fail to perceive the true nature, the "giftness" of these things that give us life, afford us pleasure, provide us with meaning, and keep us in relationship with one another—and with the entire universe—on a daily basis. They are so frequently discounted when we evaluate our assets, tally our achievements, and assess the quality of our lives in terms of material wealth, physical security, and basic comfort.

The Negative Gifts

Let's talk a moment about the negative gifts, the difficult places in our lives that have eventually turned out to be opportunities of growth for us. Can you think of any in your own life? When I began talking about this at a retreat I was giving, I happened to say that even the death of someone we love can be gift to us. This was received with fury by most of the people in the group, who challenged me to give an example of this. I replied that the death of my own father, which in fact was a negative event, was and still is a source of gift to me.

When I was thirteen he was diagnosed as having cancer of the larynx. Because of his need to use his voice in his job as a stockbroker, he refused surgery to have his voice-box removed and opted for radiation therapy. For the next two years he fought the cancer tooth and nail, refusing to admit that he was getting thinner and thinner on a daily basis. When people came to visit him, he would say "I'm going to lick this!" It was agonizing to realize that this would not happen for him. It also created a barrier of communication between him, my mother, myself, and his friends, for we had to keep up a cheerful pretense that sooner or later everything would be all right.

Then one day, about six months before his death, a friend of his from the St. Vincent de Paul Society, to which he belonged, came to visit and confronted him with the fact that he was not going to get better. From that point on he prepared himself to die. Communication lines opened. He was able to say good-by to my mother and myself. He was able to give me all the advice he wanted me to have for a lifetime of living. He became joyful again. He grew spiritually as he was able to talk about his faith and what it had come to mean to him in the previous five years. He was looking forward to whatever God had in store for him after death. This I saw, day after day, for six months—a man who looked forward to the vision of God, a man in whom Christ was being born in each suffering minute. This was his gift to me, a gift that would not have been able to be given if he had not died in this way.

The fact that he died was certainly not, per se, the gift. No suffering in itself is or ever will be gift. The gift was found by looking for the gift of meaning in that event. During the days of his dying he taught me what was most important in life. He also modeled the way in which I myself would like to die. All tragedies, all negative events can be transformed into gift if we have the desire to become aware of the gift. This does not mean that we glibly deny the pain and suffering. It means that we allow ourselves to experience it completely, become aware of all of it, acknowledge it, accept it, then go beyond it to a new meaning. Most of the time we will never know why something happened. But we can always open ourselves to something we need to learn from the event.

After I related this story, one of the participants raised her hand and asked to speak. She said, "I hated you when you first talked about the gift in negative events, for I have just lost my six-year-old only grandson to leukemia. But then, as you were talking, I realized that he has been gift to us all for six wonderful years. We have not owned him, he always belonged to God, even if we didn't fully realize that. Somehow, the thought of him as a temporary, lovely gift is consoling."

Being Aware of Gift

How aware are you of the gifts you have received over the course of your lifetime? Do you live in a state of conscious awareness of your past and present gifts? Are you most aware of your past gifts and do you find yourself dwelling on those that have been lost or taken away? We are called to keep the blessings of God ever in our minds. Most of us don't. Most of us don't even see the abundance of gifts around us, awaiting our recognition on a daily basis.

As someone who had, over the years, slipped into the habit of low-grade but chronic dissatisfaction and too frequent complaining about everything from the price of meat in China to my excess weight, this exercise of "looking for the gift" after my accident was not an easy task for me to undertake, and it required a tremendous amount of effort and energy. I was so used to ignoring even the "big stuff." I had conditioned myself for many years to believe that I needed more and more complex things, activities, or achievements to make me and other people happy.

One Wednesday morning early in this exercise I drove into the parking lot at work, about two minutes late for a faculty meeting. I was annoyed because I had been delayed by traffic, but knew that I could still be "acceptably late" if I hurried. I jumped out of the car and raced through the dew-wet grass to the back door of our building, hoping to slip into the meeting unnoticed. The door—which was never locked—was locked. All kinds of words came to my mind, and I was inordinately annoyed, mainly because now I was going to have to walk completely around the building, about the length of a city block! Not only that, but even though it was 7:30 in the morning, it was Indian summer in Louisville, and the day was already steamy hot. I was going to get sweaty!

To add insult to injury, I was wearing high heels, even though I had a friction blister on my heel from those same shoes, and my foot hurt for distance walking. And so on and so on went the complaints. Then, suddenly, I caught myself and remembered that I was trying to find gift in daily life. Surely there's no gift here. Too bad, must report this whole idea just doesn't fit reality. It was a nice thought while it lasted. Then, as I turned the corner of the building, allowing myself to slow down as I realized I could not control the situation, I opened my eyes and looked one more time. What I saw in that moment was the lightness of the fall morning sunshine, the most intense, cloudless blue sky, kelly green grass with droplets of dew that reflected the sun like crystal, and a very large, dark, and beautiful black woman wearing a bright pink cotton jumpsuit. What struck my consciousness at that moment and all at once, was the gift of *color*. Amazing!

All day long I remained conscious of color. I'm not an artist, so color isn't one of my areas of particular concern or expertise. But suddenly I became aware that everything had a color. Some color was lovely, some was not, but the recognition of color was intense and a true joy to my senses that stayed with me for the entire day. Even now, I continue to be much more aware of and appreciative of the gift of color. Needless to say, in the enjoyment of the experience, I forgot about the complaints I had, and no one even realized or cared that I was a few minutes late for the meeting.

If all that exists is *not* gift to you, what is it that keeps you from seeing your own existence and everything in it—body, mind, family, friends, food, education, work, talents, religion—the earth itself—as gift? Why do you not constantly sing within your heart the psalm blessing Yahweh for the many kindnesses you have been given? Could it be that you—as I had not—have never really "looked" at all of this as gift? Have you taken for granted most of what you have actually been given? Do you believe that you are the person responsible for providing yourself with these things? Have you bought into the American myth, the old Horatio Alger story that you must be a self-made person to be of any value in this society?

Have you made of yourself your own creator? Most of us do believe that we are the cause of our lives, because the prevailing mindset is that we are independent people, capable of taking care of ourselves. We may briefly recognize God as the first and primary source of our gifts, but by and large, we put more emphasis on and give more credit to ourselves for having responded to and used these gifts than to being aware of and grateful for the gifts themselves. Granted, we do respond and create gifts of our own for ourselves and others, but the bottom line is that who we are and what we have and experience are ultimately pure gifts of the Creator God who is both the origin and giver of all that is.

The belief that I am the creator of my own life brings deep grief and a tremendous sense of frustration when I can no longer provide what I want for myself. Consider this question for a moment. Throughout your life, have you tended to pay more attention to what you don't have than to what you do have? Has your glass always been half full or half empty? As you have advanced in years, have you found yourself paying more attention to the loss of your gifts than to the gifts you still enjoy? Do you think more about your deficits than your assets? Do you worry that the assets you do have will be taken away? Have you lost hope that God will continue to shower you with gifts, even though these may be gifts of another kind—new ones, different kinds, gifts that will accompany you through very old age, declining abilities, and death?

You certainly may choose to look at life in the old, independent, self-made way. That is the narcissistic, grandiose, and humanly isolating premise on which most of our global societies function; so on one level that view of reality will be easier to live out. But you are a Christian. And as a Christian you are called—for the first time in the history of humankind—to create a new vision, a different mindset, for later life, a new way of seeing yourself and everyone else. You are called to open your eyes and examine what is around you, slowly, calmly, deliberately, peacefully, lovingly. You are called to see what you have been given so that you can enjoy it fully in a spirit of humility, appreciation, and gratefulness.

For there is always more—much, much more to which you are constantly being invited. Your Father has called you into being to experience, to share an incredible, perpetually expanding abundance of life—God's own life lived in loving unity with the Son and the Spirit. This abundance of life is not given as our society gives—just to children and young adults. God's abundance is for all ages, for all stages of the life span. God wants to gift you, to energize you, with this abundance. God wants to pour into you each second of each day of your life gifts that will ravish you, that will sweep you off your feet, that will envelop you with love and joy and peace. God's great anguish comes from your barriers— your inability or refusal to become aware that these gifts exist for you. They are there for you: there for the asking and for the receiving.

3

❦

AWARENESS

Now instead of the spirit of the world, we have received the Spirit that comes from God, to teach us to understand the gifts that he has given us.

1 Corinthians 2:12

YOU MIGHT BE SAYING TO YOURSELF, "I DON'T DO SO BADLY, I'm pretty satisfied with my life, I know nothing's perfect, so why should I change the way I look at life, especially if it is counter to society in general? Who needs more problems? Anyway, how can I change the way I look at things? What I see is what I see. I'm practical, a realist; this 'new vision' stuff is not for me. And another thing—what I see is not all gift—much of my life and everyone else's is filled with pain, misery, suffering, boredom, with the gifts few and far between. That Thibault woman is nuts! Get real, lady."

I'll say right now that there certainly is no worldly reason to change your way of seeing, your vision of reality, if you are totally content with it, if it fits your biological, psychological, intellectual, emotional, interpersonal, and spiritual needs at this time. If it ain't broke, don't fix it! No, as I said in the introduction, I am writing for the spiritually discontent, those who are looking for the something more but don't really know what it is and where it may be found. Only those people will be open to attempting to look at life differently because what they have now is no longer working;

they are the poor in spirit. People who are content feel no pressure to change or alter themselves or their lives in any way. And that's fine, as long as they are still growing in the love of one another. When the growth of love becomes stagnant, then it's time to take a new look at one's life. (Even if you're feeling happy and contented, you might want to try out a few new ways of looking at things, some "awareness" exercises just for a little excitement!)

Being Vigilant

Awareness is an interesting phenomenon. We can't become aware of something unless we are somehow clued into the fact that it exists. This clue or information is a gift in itself and usually comes from a source outside of ourselves, from another person, the media, reading, observation of events, etc. In addition to having information that something exists, we must want to connect with it, to enter into relationship with it in some way. To do this we must first be "ready" for the awareness—ready physically, intellectually, emotionally, morally, and spiritually. The seed must fall on fertile ground. But what is it that facilitates the connection between readiness (a state of discontent) and the object of awareness? I think the bridge between a gift and our awareness of it is the state of *vigilance*. Vigilance is an intense psychological state of wakefulness, alertness, watchfulness, and sleeplessness. When one is vigilant, one desires something, watches for it, and is ready and able to accept it when it is given, just as the "wise virgins" of Jesus' parable were (see Matt. 25:1-13).

So the process goes like this. First we must be informed or learn in some way that there is something good available to us—a gift. Then we must desire to become *aware* of its presence, wherever and whenever it shows up. In the next step we must ask for the awareness of the gift, acknowledging the fact that we can't force ourselves to become aware, that it is something that "happens" to us. Then we must become vigilant—open to receiving what we're looking for—and, equally important, we must actually believe that we're going to be gifted with what we're looking for.

In the previous chapter, I talked about wanting to see the gift in my being late and having the office door locked. In that situation I became vigilant—I stopped everything I was doing, turned all of my attention for a few seconds on *what I wanted more than anything else,* and then *asked* for the awareness. I then let go of my attempts to control or create my awareness. This "letting go" allowed my mind to become psychologically relaxed enough to receive awareness of whatever the gift was to be—in this case, the joyful awareness of color. It was also an act of faith, arising from the belief that God really desires my constant awareness of these gifts given to me. The bottom line is that you have to want it, then ask for it, then relax and open your eyes and expect to get it! This process is nothing more than the "ask and you will receive" lesson that Jesus taught (Matt. 7:7).

Let's look at a very mundane way in which this awareness process works in everyday life, on an accidental basis. Do you remember the last time you bought a car? If you're anything like me, you were probably overwhelmed by the variety of models, makes, and colors that exist in the car world today. It took you a while to decide which one you wanted, and in what color. You chose a car that you hadn't even realized existed before because you were content with your old, comfy, familiar auto. You had no need to be attentive to everything on four wheels that passed you. So you leave the dealer's showroom and drive home. Lo and behold, what do you see but seven cars of the same make speeding down the expressway. And three of them are wearing the same color, the exact shade of magenta you chose! Isn't that amazing?

Believe it or not, they were all there before you became aware of them. And they didn't congregate on the highway in some mystical manner to demonstrate to you how wise your choice was. They were around before you became aware of their existence, but you had no need, no interest, no desire to see them—they were part of the background of your life. It was only when you developed a desire for a new car, ventured out to obtain information about what existed, and made a commitment to what you wanted more than any other model, that this tremendous awareness of car-dom assaulted you, and in particular, the awareness of one specific car among many.

Knowing what we want or need, then desiring, asking, being receptive, and believing we will be given what we are looking for is the way we become conscious of the realities around us. This is the process by which we become aware of all things in the material, psychological, interpersonal, artistic, and spiritual domains. This process is the key to our awareness of all things.

Another example is that of the new mother, and you may have experienced this yourself. Before her child is born a pregnant woman, if she is comfortable enough to sleep at night and is a sound sleeper, can theoretically sleep the night through without being awakened even by a noisy thunderstorm. The minute her child comes home from the hospital, however, she is alert to the tiniest whimper, even while she is sound asleep. As soon as she hears even a change in breathing pattern, she may be jumping out of bed to see if the baby is all right. It appears as if she has developed a new and highly acute sense of hearing. In actuality her hearing has not changed. She desires with both body and mind to be aware of her child's need for her in the night, and thus her whole being is attuned to and can respond to the cry.

I have spouses of persons with Alzheimer's disease who tell me that they experience this intensity of awareness as caregivers. The ability to engage in this kind of awareness on a level of biological reality is essential to the survival of the human being.

And, finally, have you ever gone into a library or bookstore, knowing you needed some advice, some new awareness of what life was all about, and had just the book you needed to read almost fall off the shelf onto your head? This happens to me a great deal and, unfortunately, I am in great credit card debt due to my too-frequent trips to our local bookstores!

Widening Our Vision

Very important also is the fact that we have been given the freedom to choose what we see, what we pay attention to, what we rest our awareness on. There are zillions of things that can attract us, call us to themselves. Our task is to choose which ones we want to pay attention to, which ones we want to invest our energy in, for we cannot endure full consciousness of everything. We must focus on something more limited.

On the other hand, we must not be too narrow in our awareness. We must be careful not to develop a preconceived idea of what we want the gift to be. Then it would not be gift, it would be something we went out and shopped for deliberately. (That's no fun; we have to do that on an almost daily basis, anyway!) No, we must always be expecting a surprise—a gift that is wrapped up in paper, hidden from immediate view.

How do we come to a balance between total awareness and the too-limited view? It takes some practice. For most of us the difficulty will be in the widening of our vision. To do this we might start by spending a few minutes—no more than a couple at the beginning—just becoming aware of our surroundings. Most of the time we rarely see or hear what is actually within our range of perception. To become conscious of the way you filter out awareness, try this exercise:

(1) Stop what you are doing—the activity that is absorbing the greater part of your mind—reading this book, for example. Look around you and note what you both see and hear.

(2) Take a deep breath and hold it for three seconds. Breathe out slowly, and repeat this twice. This will help you to relax a little. When we're anxious we become narrowly focused on just a few things we mull over and over. Relaxation allows our minds to be receptive to the awareness of much more.

(3) For a full minute look all around you, slowly resting your eyes on one thing, then going to the next. Just let things be in your vision. Be aware of the mental commentary you make

on them; most of this commentary will be judgmental. (Is that table ever dusty! and so forth.) If you can, just let your mind wander instead of creating thoughts.

(4)   Listen to the sounds around you. What do you hear?

When you have finished, ask yourself two questions. What did I see and what did I hear that I had not seen or heard before? How did my mind with its constant need to form thoughts about and to judge what I saw and heard interfere with or obstruct my ability to see and hear?

This exercise is also a good way to become aware of our bodies. We tend to concentrate our consciousness, our thoughts, on a few parts that are worrying us, that give us some pain or limit us in some way, neglecting the rest of the body, which may be desperate for attention. Here is a simple body awareness exercise:

(1)   Stop. Get into a comfortable position.
(2)   Deep breathe three times.
(3)   Starting with the very top of your head, traveling down to the tip of your toes, scan your body mentally. Be aware of your head—eyes, ears, nose, skin, scalp, etc. How do they feel? Hot? Cold? Painful? Pleasant? Numb? Do this with each portion of your body.
(4)   Be aware of the judgmental comments your mind makes about each of your body parts.
(5)   What feelings or sensations are you aware of that you had not been conscious of before you did this exercise?

You may have become a little more aware of how you filter out a good deal of reality in your everyday life. We tend to have a preconceived notion of what we will find in our field of vision and hearing and sensing. This preconceived notion blocks out our awareness of other things. A truly spiritual task, a discipline actually, is to take the time as often as possible each day to stop, look, and listen to whatever is around and within us. Just a minute or so four or five times a day will gradually lead us into a heightened awareness of what is truly around us and within us.

4

❦

GREED

Let your thoughts be on heavenly things, not on the things that are on the earth, because you have died, and now the life you have is hidden with Christ in God. . . . That is why you must kill everything in you that belongs only to earthly life: fornication, impurity, guilty passion, evil desires and especially greed, which is the same thing as worshipping a false god.

Colossians 3:2-3, 5

JEANNETTE IS AN ELDERLY WOMAN WHO WAS BROUGHT BY HER family to me for counseling. She was suffering from arthritis, which interfered with her ability to manage her household and take care of her personal needs. She was ninety-one years old and had been fiercely independent all of her life.

Her family still told stories—legends, really—of how she had run away from home at eleven years of age and had made a successful life for herself as a seamstress, tailor, then, ultimately, a women's clothing manufacturer. She was a "self-made" woman. Over the years she had amassed considerable wealth. Now she lived by herself in a twelve-room home greatly in need of repair. She was no longer able to cook and clean and take care of her personal hygiene, and, due to physical pain, had become overwhelmed by bills and other financial concerns. Yet she refused all but the most minimal help.

She would only allow Meals on Wheels to bring her a lunch five days a week. Her family—a daughter who was an older woman herself and three nieces and nephews—were distraught. They took turns visiting and ensuring her welfare, cleaning her house, trying to sort out her life and keep her safe, trying to convince her to either have someone live with her or go to a retirement home. Finally, it seemed that a considerable part of each of their days was spent enabling her to live just as she had lived in her earlier years. They were pulled into her greed for independence and control, and their lives were being negatively affected by it.

What do I mean by criticizing this independent woman? Shouldn't we try to keep older individuals in their homes as long as we can? How dare I say that she is greedy—she's maintaining her sense of independence, and we can't take that away from her! The socially prevalent and acceptable thinking is that we should do everything in our power to maintain her "independent" lifestyle.

To say that she is motivated by greed, however, is far too simplistic an explanation of this woman's behavior, for she was certainly physically impaired and fearful for her very life. However, I do assert that it was a lifelong attitude, a general orientation to greed that caused her to get into this predicament. Because she wants what she wants, when she wants it, and in the manner that she desires it, she clings to what was good and pleasurable for her in the past and cannot let go of it. This house no longer serves her needs, yet because of her attachment to it, she is not free to let it go and experience the gift that a well-run retirement community might be to her. She is hurting others who have become very tired and frustrated in their caretaking roles, yet she is unable to be empathic with their situation. At this time, she is full of fear, for she has lost the will to visualize what a change in environment might mean for her, how it might improve her satisfaction in life. Had she adopted a gift mentality years ago she might be able, even in her pain, to let go of the gift of the house to be able to accept the gift of community with others.

Greed may seem to be a harsh word to use for the little comforts we allow ourselves. We tend to think of greed as a characteristic of young and middle-aged adult "yuppie" life, where people are intent on amassing as much stuff and as many pleasurable experiences as they can. However, in my daily work as a clinical gerontologist assessing, treating, and counseling older adults and their families, I all too often see the aftermath of lives like Jeannette's, tainted by the illusions and seductions of greed.

Greed in the Garden

I enjoy playing around with the myth of Creation, especially the Garden of Eden scenario. One story line I like to imagine is that God created all manner of things for these human folk, but also had some other, off-limits "stuff" that human folk were not to be concerned with. The things for the human folk were wonderful—magnificent—more than they could ever imagine wanting, needing, or using. And all of it was pure gift to them from their own Creator. But the human folk did not see the giftness of what they were given. They could not actually see their God, so they did not see God's power and might and love. They also thought that, since God was so friendly and intimate with them, they had a right to everything God had, including the other things that were not supposed to be gift to them. Because they lacked the gift mindset, they just helped themselves to what they thought was their right. And we have been doing that ever since.

The taking of things that are not ours, that belong to someone else, is called greed. It is what motivates all of us at some times and in varying degrees in this society. It is a source of great want, tremendous desire, the feeling of all-encompassing deprivation, loneliness, isolation. It is the root of all addictions. Basically, greed is nothing more than a lack of trust in a gifting God, a fear that God will not provide us with enough of what we need. And, as a result, it is a settling for *less* than we were called to be given.

What are you greedy for? Are you aware of what you want versus what you need? Are you unwilling to let anything go? Here's a test. If God granted you the gift of living to be 115 years old, would you accept it as a blessing or a curse? Most people I pose this question to shudder when they imagine themselves surviving to this age. Their first reaction is usually that they would not want to live that long. Then, after a little thought a few will admit they might like to live that long "as long as I still have my mind and can do what I want to do when I want to do it, with very little physical discomfort."

Isn't this the attitude most of us have most of the time about everything in our lives? We want (1) what we want (2) when we want it (3) in the manner or mode in which we want it presented to us, and (4) we don't want to suffer or pay too dearly for it. In addition, if we get what we want we quickly forget where it comes from, only occasionally share it, and very rarely relinquish it when the time comes to give it up.

Greed for Activity

A major source of greed in later life is in the area of activity. Have you ever noticed retired friends say "I'm busier now that I'm retired than I ever was while I was working. Just don't know where the time goes!" Is this true of your own life? Are you on a merry-go-round of daily activities that leave you no time for yourself? Are you constantly doing committee work, volunteer activities, traveling, babysitting, card playing? Do you feel compelled to engage in these activities because you feel that your life would have no meaning if your days weren't filled to the brim with activity? Do you feel guilty when you have more than a few hours in which you have nothing to do? Do all of these things you have to do satisfy you deeply, or do you find yourself wishing you weren't involved in quite so much?

Our society today is frenetically active. There is less and less time for the quieting of the heart and mind, for calming down. Less time available for "just being" with ourselves and with those who are close to us, in whose company we are nurtured. The sign of the times that one is truly "important" is the quality and size of the appointment calendar.

48

Greed for Information

We feel compelled to keep informed. We are constantly being bombarded with information via television, radio, newspaper, magazines, memos, mail, and telephone calls, most of which is trivial and unnecessary. (Who cares that today is Paul Newman's sixty-something birthday—glad he's made it this long, but I don't need to know the details!) Yet, if we don't stay on top of it, we somehow feel anxious, afraid that we are missing something.

There are more substantial things to learn as well. I sit here at the kitchen table (nastily early in the morning because this is the only time I can find that's at all undisturbed, and even then two irresistible cats are clamoring for a scratch), writing with a new laptop computer bought just for this purpose by my computer-literate husband. On this awesome machine I have mastered only the barebones functions—how to turn it on, how to pick up the appropriate file called "My Book," how to type, and how to turn it off. Downstairs in my study I have a regular, larger computer with a printer which was bought six years ago. I can't do any more on that one, for the same reason! Yet I feel guilty, because in my profession I must be "computer literate." I go around knowing that any day now someone will discover that I am illiterate, and I will be hastily sent off, kicking and screaming, to computer school! Sometimes I find myself yearning for retirement and get jealous of older adults who have made it to that point.

Yet, when I take a good look at their lives, very many of them are living in nearly the same way. They have lived full, busy lives and feel great pressure to keep those lives just as full with endless things to do. One woman wailed to me, "I have so many commitments and don't feel free to get out of any of them—I might as well be working and earning money for all this work!"

Greed for Respect

What is all this activity about, anyway? Why do we feel compelled to be *doing* all of the time? The answer is fairly simple. The society that has developed out of our material, sensory world requires us to be financially productive before it will allow us any sense of honor and prestige, or even respect. That's the bottom line. The more you do, the more money you bring in, the more you show you have money by buying the things that let folks know that you can afford it, the more socially acceptable, the more worthy of being loved you will be. This is an incredibly strong and powerful message, one that is hard to counter. It even spills over into volunteer work after retirement. I have seen people who feel so guilty about the fact that they are no longer contributing financially at home and in the workplace that they fill every waking hour with volunteer activities to compensate for their basic feelings of poor self-worth. They do not experience the gift of life—their own life—for its own sake. They think that the more they do the more they will be loved.

Greed for R & R

Another area of greed is manifested in just the opposite way—deciding that we have done enough, deserve rest and recreation for the remainder of our days, and then drop out of all concern for the society around us. This is greed for one's own time with great reluctance to share this time with or for anyone else. Frequently people who have been so busy *doing* burn out or get disenchanted when they are not recognized or praised enough for what they do. The age for this kind of time greed is getting earlier and earlier. Retirement in the mid-fifties or even younger is not uncommon. Most of these early retirees go on to new projects and involvements, but many do not, spending almost half of their lives playing and otherwise entertaining themselves.

Greed to Be the Giver

Another area of greed that I have observed is the need to be the giver rather than the receiver in a relationship. The conflict between the desire to be the giver and the need to be the recipient sometimes culminates in a crisis of identity in the later years. People who have seen themselves as givers, contributors to society, and builders of new programs, often create a sense of self that is off-balance. Their sense of self-esteem comes only from the feeling of giving to others. Sometimes they give so much that they rob others of the opportunity to enjoy giving! They feel they are judged on the basis of how much they have given. They interpret "Love thy neighbor" to mean "give" to thy neighbor, without realizing that to love means both to give and to receive—allowing the other person to give. They also enjoy the admiration of people who observe their generosity and praise them for it. It is really the praise to which they are addicted, for they cannot praise themselves; they do not know how to love themselves.

Greed for recognition and praise for giving can be a primary source of anguish in later life when something—perhaps ill health—prevents persons from giving and forces them into the role of the receiver. I am reminded of one elderly man, a major philanthropist, who said, in tears, "I am used to giving, rather than receiving. Now I have to receive charity. And it hurts; it is intolerable. I would rather be dead!"

Many people express their aversion and fears about having to receive rather than give by saying that they are willing to live into very old age only if they retain all their functions and do not become a burden to their families. Yet these people fully and happily accepted the burden that their families were to them in earlier years! What is the problem? In addition to the desire for praise, it is also an issue of power. When you give, you are powerful and you have the upper hand. When you receive, you are at the mercy of another, who now has the upper hand. In this society, we are not allowed to be in power simultaneously—only one person or group can have the position of power, which is definitely the preferred position. So we go through our lives fearing the time when we will have diminished power over our own lives and the lives of others.

And the fear itself diminishes us.

Did not Jesus say to Peter, after Peter had objected to Jesus' washing his feet, "Unless I wash you, you will have no share with me" (John 13:8, NRSV)?

We, also, must learn to relinquish power, to allow our feet to be washed—perhaps literally!

5

DISCONTENT

What shall I do, that I may find my God?
"The invisible things of God being understood by the things made"
(Romans 1:20). I will consider the earth and its great beauty; I
marvel at the greatness of the sea; I look up and behold the
heavens, and gaze upon the beauty of the stars; I wonder at the
splendor of the sun and moon. Yet, although I praise these things—
for Him who made them, I thirst.

Saint Augustine, *Sermons*

LET'S GET BACK TO CATHERINE, THE PERSON I INTRODUCED at the beginning of the book, a woman who has everything by the world's standards—health, intelligence, wealth, family, friends, interesting activities, lovely possessions. Catherine has gathered and stocked up more and more of this "stuff" around her as she has aged. Yet, she hasn't been outwardly greedy; on the contrary, she has been very generous with her goods. She supports well her favorite charities, and they are many. She has led an exemplary, well-disciplined life. She has been self-sacrificingly active in her church. She has satisfying relationships with a number of caring friends.

Yet even with all of these good things, something is missing from Catherine's life. She feels that there is more "out there" for her to buy or to do, but she doesn't know where to go, what she needs, or what it is she must do. Despite all of her wealth, she feels empty. She is discontent and wants something, but she doesn't know what that something is. What *is* it that will fill her emptiness? How can she move beyond this painful discontent?

The answer to these questions comes from within, for Catherine and also for those of us who feel the same sense of emptiness and discontent.

Acknowledging Our Giftedness

In order to begin to move out of this painful state we have a spiritual decision to make. Most of us will be confronted with the need to make this decision some time after mid-life. (We are called to make it early in life, but it is very difficult for most of us to do completely in the younger years, given the demands of daily survival in today's society.) We need to decide, once and for all, whether we are willing to acknowledge that we are totally gifted people, sustained and nurtured and developed by gift—by the graciousness of God—or whether we will continue to choose to believe that through our independent efforts we are the source of our own existence and well-being. This decision will require an intentional act of the will, a "conversion," a freely-chosen change of mindset from greed to gift.

The acknowledgment that is called for here is an admission of our intrinsic poverty, our basic emptiness, coupled with trust that we will be filled to the brim and overflowing. We are totally dependent on gift and our need to be open to receiving the gifts of God in order to be maintained physically, emotionally, socially, and spiritually. We are dependent on gift to live the "abundant life" as a small but significant part of all Creation.

The Results of This Decision

Once made, the decision to recognize and acknowledge our basic poverty, our empty-handedness before God, will cause a number of things to happen. We will experience an increasing "letting go" of our small-minded, egocentric selves. We will become interested in life beyond the self. We will begin to abandon the belief that we are invulnerable. We will forget all ideas we have ever entertained that we are our own creators. This does not mean that we relinquish responsibility for our actions, our self-care, and our creativity. In fact, we become even more responsible and creative. It does mean that we will adopt a growing attitude of inner openness and simplicity.

Once we become aware of and acknowledge the gift-nature of our lives we will begin to turn radically toward God with increasingly open hearts, minds, and hands. Trusting in the benevolence of God's love, perhaps for the first time, we will tentatively start to allow ourselves to be loved. A childlike openness to God and all the gifts God desires to give us and to others through us will become our new life stance.

We will be led into new and unknown territory—the territory of the life of the Spirit, who is the Giver of life. We will become much more sensitive to and appreciative of the gifts of our old age. Rather than seeing later life as a time of loss, the focus will be placed on what we are constantly being given.

The Inner Gifts of Later Life

The gifts provided us in later life are many and varied. They are given to us in all of the realms of experience—the physical, intellectual, emotional, and interpersonal. They may include good health and the ability to function as we like, grandchildren, leisure, the opportunity to spend time as we see fit, the opportunity to travel, to obtain more education at very little cost, to do volunteer work, to engage in some artistic, creative activity, to do what we *really* want to do perhaps for the first time in our lives.

There are other gifts that are not as externally obvious and may not even be looked upon as gifts when seen out of the eyes of greed. They are inner gifts, gifts of character, gifts that make us truly human. The ability to endure pain and disability with a cheerful smile for the benefit of others. Courage in the face of loss. The desire to reach out to help others when one's own loneliness is almost overwhelming. The refusal to withdraw from another when that person is increasingly ravaged by the results of Alzheimer's disease and is becoming insensitive or even abusive.

Marjorie is a good example of a person with such inner gifts. She lost her husband of fifty-four years very unexpectedly. He had been in good health one day and in the hospital, never to return, the next. After a month in intensive care he died, leaving her with tremendous bills due to inadequate insurance. Her only child, a son, lived eighteen hours away and could not help very much. Within one week of her bereavement she had to place an older and much-loved sister into a nursing home, due to Alzheimer's disease. Two weeks later, her other sister's health failed and she had to go to her, to help her take care of a slightly retarded, elderly, diabetic brother who lived with her.

To the outward eye Marjorie had an overwhelming amount of loss and difficulty to deal with. Yet, upon visiting with her I found her inwardly joyful. She was sad, yes, and realistically in touch with her losses, but she continued to respond in a caring way to the life with which she was entrusted. She cried when she remembered her husband, yet she admitted to being sustained by a sense of his presence and continuing care. She admitted that her sister's existence in the nursing home saddened her, but she continued to be concerned about how she could make that existence more peaceful. She recognized that her diabetic brother was becoming increasingly debilitated and at some point would not be able to give himself his insulin. So Marjorie, at the age of eighty, after having been exceedingly squeamish all of her life, learned to give injections.

These are gifts of the inner spirit. Marjorie is aware of them and acknowledges that she is not the source of these gifts. She is also aware of having made, a few years back, the decision to see life "as a glass half full," as she puts it. This is another way of saying that she chooses to celebrate the gifts of her life instead of bemoaning the inevitable losses. The inspiring way she lives her life, despite its pain, is gift in itself to those who know her.

We are all called to translate the events of our lives as gift in later life. Our specific situations will differ, but our response can be the same. And the results for our lives—peace and joy—can be as great as they are for Marjorie.

6

❧

THE GIFT OF GIFTS

No man ever wanted anything so much as God wants to make the soul aware of him. God is ever ready, but we are so unready. God is in, we are out; God is at home, we are strangers.

Meister Eckhart, *Sermons*

BACK TO CATHERINE. DO YOU REMEMBER WHAT SHE FINALLY became aware of? She began to realize that her emptiness and discontent arose from her inability to "connect" with God. She said to me, "I know what it is I want—and nothing else will do. I want to experience God. It seems as though I've been behaving well and working for someone I've read and heard about, and have respected and feared, but have never met in person and have never really known and loved. Well, it's high time we met! Where do I go from here?"

With these words Catherine was asking for the gift of God's Self—the gift of such a total relationship that God could be present to her and she to God in a mutually-enjoyed, shared life that has no ending and gets better and better as time goes on. What a request! Is it possible? Yes!

Above and beyond the many lovely gifts we are given on a daily basis, there is one primary, all-encompassing "Gift of Gifts," which God desires more than anything else to lavish on us. There really is no greater gift than this except for the full enjoyment of God after death, and this gift is a preview of those things to come.

The gift I am speaking of here is a gift of the Spirit. It is given to us in three parts. These three parts include:

1)   the gift of the indwelling presence of God;
2)   the gift of our own, ever-increasing human ability to become aware of this presence; and
3)   the gift of the ability to share the joy of living in this presence with other people in "blessed community."

The Gift of God's Indwelling Presence

The first part is the actual giving of God's Self to us—God's life within us, the gift of the loving presence of the Father/Mother-Creator, Son/Lover-Teacher, and Spirit/Energizer-Guide abiding within each of us, available to us as a sharing of their life. Christ promised this gift to his disciples, and through them, to each of us when he said:

> If anyone loves me he will keep my word, and my Father will love him, and we shall come to him and make our home with him.
>
> John 14:23

This means that if we reach out in love to other people, abiding by Christ's instructions on how to love effectively, then God has promised to come and dwell among us and within us and to be present in love to us at all times. The kingdom—the realm, the reality—of God is above us and below us and all around us, yes. The kingdom is also within us. We are living within the All that is God and this All enfolds and encompasses all that we are, down to the most minute of the subatomic particles that compose our bodies.

There is no actual distinction between God within and God without, but we want to concentrate here on the experience of God within, God's nearness to us. Too often we experience only the distance between God and ourselves. When we concentrate on distance, God then becomes so "Other" that we can't imagine ourselves reaching for and contacting God, whether within or without. But even the presence of God within, incredible as it may be, is just the first part of the gift.

The Gift of Becoming Aware of God's Presence

As if that were not enough in itself, the second part of this gift is that we are invited and have been given the capacity to become continually and consciously aware of—to know, and to experience, and to enjoy—this loving presence of the Father, Son, and Spirit within. We are called to become wide awake to the fact that we have the potential to live in complete unity of loving relationship with God. Right now—at this time and in this place. This awareness of participating in love is incredibly life-enhancing—it *is* life; it is our reason for being. But this gift is still not the end of the story.

The Gift of Sharing God's Presence

The third part of the gift of God's presence is that, once we are aware of it in our own lives, we are asked to share it with other people—*all* other people. The nice thing about this part is that once we are aware of such Presence we can hardly keep ourselves from sharing it, even if we wanted to. We are meant to live such shared life in "Blessed Community" (Thomas Kelly, *Testament of Devotion*) with one another. We are meant to share on very deep, "real" levels. Unfortunately, more often than not, we remain on the surface of things in our relationships with other people. We stay isolated, distant. We keep to ourselves. We stay uninvolved most of the time. We take care of number one.

Most of us are starved for the real presence of one another. Take a look at the number of books published that deal with communication and the problems of communication—communication between husbands and wives, males and females, employers and employees. Communication seems to be our most significant problem these days. Why? Because we do not know how to be present to one another in a real sharing of who we are.

We put up masks; we act parts that we think others expect us to be. Many of us act so much we have lost touch with who we really are. We can no longer even be present to ourselves.

Entrance into the awareness of God's presence to us teaches us how to be present to ourselves and then to one another. The greatest gift we can give to another person is the gift of our total presence, our ability to "be with" that person. Think about it. Have you experienced recently anyone *being there* for you? Totally engrossed in what you were saying? Totally "with" you and not distracted by thoughts of his or her own?

If so, you were very fortunate. Most of us experience this, if at all, only rarely. And most of us do not allow ourselves to be present to others completely, either. Yet, when it does happen, we feel so good! We know we have been accepted for who we are; we know we don't have to put energy into acting a part, we don't have to defend ourselves. We are liberated to become who we really are. It is the best of all gifts from one person to another. This is what Jesus meant when he told us to "Love one another." He wasn't telling us to do things for one another while staying uninvolved. We are to enter into shared presence with one another. And this is the hardest of all things to do for most of us who don't even know how to be with ourselves.

If we were able to be present to one another in such a sharing of the heart, we would never again feel ourselves to be "orphans." Yes, there would be lonely moments when this sharing was not available, but we would be comforted by the remembrance that it has happened, it does exist, and it will come again. For this is what the risen Christ is. This kind of relationship, this depth of presence is what Christ died trying to show us how to enter into. This *is* the kingdom of God on earth.

Aware of God Within

I have been challenged by a few people who argue that it doesn't make any difference whether we become aware of God within or outside of us, as long as we become aware of God in some way.

They claim that the transcendence or "otherness" of God is adequate and that this way of being with God is probably most in keeping with an innate personality type. The message is "leave these folks alone; don't upset them if they can't experience God within, or as 'immanent.' Respect their personality type, the way they are."

I've given this a great deal of thought and prayer. My response is that we all need to try to approach the God who exists both within and without. There are many images in scripture that highlight the immensity and transcendence of God. The grandeur that is God is manifest in the vast distances of the universe and hidden in the "cloud of unknowing." This is certainly one approach to God, one that might appeal to a person who loves nature and perhaps is more comfortable in nature than in intimate relationships.

This was my orientation to God for many years, even though I yearned for a different way of being with God. This was also Catherine's way of understanding God. This is the God of the cloud and the mountain and the burning bush. The God whose face would kill you if you saw it. The God of Creation, power and might; the holy of holies; the Lord Most High; I AM; the God who has no name. This truly *is* one of the ways God manifests God's Self in the universe. Some recent writers have attempted to call this the masculine side of God. I have infinite trouble assigning masculine and feminine traits to God, so I will take the liberty of disagreeing with them, saying that this is one way our finite minds understand God's manifestation in time and place.

I believe that the manifestation of God as "other" was just one stage in humanity's evolving understanding of who God is, always *in relation to human beings and creation itself.* The next level in this unfolding was the assertion that God is not just "other," God is also within; God is at the center of our souls, our innermost core, our very selves. We share so much of what God is that Jesus can say, in all confidence, that our parentage is God's own Self. Just as our parents genetically live in us, so God lives in us essentially. And not only does God beget us, God also parents us, brings us up, "Abbas" us in a nurturing way.

As we become more and more aware of this essentially intimate relationship, this indwelling, we take on more and more of the attributes of God; we become transformed in the incarnate God, Christ; and we also recognize that *each and every human being has the same heritage;* each and every one is part of this body of Christ, of God. We truly are brothers and sisters of one another.

I don't think we can come to the full love of one another that Jesus was constantly urging us to enter into until we become aware that the "three-personed God" dwells within; until we recognize God within ourselves, nurturing us. Once we recognize God within, once we begin relating to the manifestation of God within and come to some awareness of spiritual and psychological "union" with God, we will begin to recognize that God also dwells in others—in those others I have been loving and those I've been hating for so many years. But if we continue to imagine an intimate scene with Christ sitting close by our side, he is still "other." As long as God is a God of outside only, we can keep him at a distance and we can keep other people at a distance.

Because it is unique to each person, the actual experience of union with God is hard to describe. It is not necessarily a physically felt or emotional sense of presence or oneness. Rather, it is a growing, intensifying, combination of total mind/body/soul awareness. It is a realization and conviction of the heart—an inner certitude that we truly are adopted children of the God who is so related to us that we are free to call God "Daddy" or "Mommy" or any other name of intimate affection. It is the concurrent realization that we live—in the here and now—in God's reality or kingdom and that we have been given all the rights and responsibilities that go with the privilege of full participation in and use of that reality. In addition, we share the kingdom's benefits equally with others—others who are in every way our brothers and sisters.

Being Truly Human

Because our lives together are such a glorious part of the kingdom, Christ taught, by his own example, what it means to be a truly human person, in relationship with other persons. He taught each one of us that being human means:

1) coming to full appreciation that you are a full-fledged child of God, who has gifted you with the kingdom and the ever-growing awareness of the gifts in it;

2) coming to an increasing awareness of the ways in which you don't know how to or refuse to live within the reality of the kingdom;

3) intensifying desire to reach out to your brothers and sisters in real sibling relationships and to help them come to awareness of their status as children a) by sharing your own awareness of being a child and b) by helping them to live lives of the kingdom-child, even if they don't recognize their status as beloved sons and daughters;

4) increasing desire and ability to act only within the truth of your life in this kingdom; and,

5) increasing desire for the spread of the truth of this kingdom to the point that you are willing to accept any and all of the consequences meted out by the unreality of life "outside" the kingdom.

Abiding by this last criterion is how Jesus got himself in trouble with the powers that were in place and then killed. The specific fact of his death on the cross is life-giving; but just as significant to me is the fact that he wanted so desperately to let us know about and to help us claim our inheritance that he grew in his willingness to be ridiculed, abandoned, tortured, and murdered for doing it. He would not back down, even though it meant his death.

We too are asked to live at this level of authenticity. We will begin to live this way when we start to become aware of the reality of our union with God. And as we grow in this awareness, at some point we will be so desirous of sharing with others, that we will also be willing to give up our lives in one way or another, if necessary, in order to be faithful to the truth of our own reality, which is life in the Reality of God.

Life in the kingdom really can be experienced in the here and now with one another. I am gifted with some friends with whom I share this kind of relationship. Each week we pray meditatively together. One evening, after spending time praying in a cozy little chapel, we lingered together in the dim light, chatting, sharing what was going on in our lives, laughing, not yet ready to leave the immense joy we found in each others' company. Another friend came by, poked his head in the door, and joked "You folks are feeding on one another!" What a perfectly accurate observation. Yes, that is exactly what we were doing—we were being fed and we were feeding, nourished by the gift of our total presence to one another. And the source of our capacity to share in such an intimate way was the vivid awareness we had of the presence of God in our own life and in the lives of the others. It was an incredibly gifted moment. And it was very affirming to have that quality of presence recognized by another person.

This was a moment of Christ's presence. It is what Christ meant when he told us to love one another. Christ knew that if we'd just risk ourselves by sharing who we are and allowing the other to share who he or she is, more often than not we'd be loved back.

"Being With" Presence

I spoke about this idea of "presence" at a workshop on spiritual growth in later life. It was held at Wesley Manor Retirement Community, and all of the residents were invited to attend. After my talk an elderly man and woman, Roger and Mary, who were both in their late eighties came up, eager to share their own story with me.

It seems that Roger, a widower, had lived at Wesley Manor for many years. He had been active in his church, but when he moved to the retirement community he decided to give up active involvement in the affairs of the church to spend time "getting to know God," as he put it. He taught himself to stay in the present moment, and he spent many hours each day just "being with" God as he walked, ate, gardened, prayed, and went around conducting his daily business. After a while he was gifted with a strong sense of God's presence nearly all the time. The care he took to be with God spilled over into his Wesley Manor relationships—he started to "be with" other people as well. Roger claimed that for the first time in his life he had stopped feeling lonely, for as he took the time to become aware of others, they, in turn, opened up to him. His once superficial relationships deepened. He even likes himself and enjoys his own company, for the first time in his life.

Now it was Mary's turn to share her story. When she first moved to Wesley Manor she was devastated at having had to leave her home, her neighborhood, her treasures. She felt this was the end of the road and that she was just marking time until death, which she hoped would be relatively soon. Then along came Roger. He had noticed her pain and knew what she was feeling because he had been through a similar experience. So he just kept her company. Didn't try to talk her out of her loneliness, her loss, her pain. He sought her out for a few minutes each day, trying not to be too obvious, and just sat with her. After a while she began sharing her pain. He let her talk. When she was ready he shared his own pain and the way he had found to deal with it. He told her how learning to "be with" God had given him a new lease on life.

Mary was at first taken aback, because she did not belong to any religion and had had no interest in things spiritual. She didn't have anything against God; she just had never given the idea of God much attention. She figured she didn't have anything to lose, so she began to try Roger's method of "being with" God. Something happened. The way Mary put it, "I've become a new woman! I feel younger, full of energy, and I'm interested in other people, in life itself for the first time in many, many years."

I smiled, thinking how wonderful it was they had entered the presence of one another through the presence of God. To my smile Mary quickly responded, "Now, I want you to know we're not lovers. We're not even in love with one another. We're just good friends who love one another deeply. I've never had a friendship like this. Somehow we know that this friendship comes from God, and we cherish it. We try to share it with the others here, too."

Sadly, most of us go through life not knowing of this invitation to enter into loving presence, not realizing our potential for such an intimately shared relationship with God and each other. Why do we not have this awareness? What keeps us from fully enjoying the presence of God to us? What keeps us from being present to God? What keeps us from being able to be present to one another?

Five things may be getting in the way of our full realization of and participation in this mutual presence. These include:

(1) *lack of awareness* of the promise that God the Father, Son, and Spirit will actually make their home within us and will be present in our consciousness if we will only reach out in love to God and others;

(2) *fear of intimacy,* which is caused by harmful, negative experiences which occurred early in our lives that have not been healed. Such experiences caused us to cope by learning harmful behaviors that can now ultimately destroy us and others. If not quite so severe, these behaviors can continue throughout our life span to interfere to a greater or lesser extent with our ability to receive love, to enjoy the fact that we truly are beloved children, and to love God and others in return. All addictive behaviors, from alcoholism to workaholism, fall into this category.

(3) *deliberate refusal to pay attention* to the significance of this gift due to our greed for other things, which causes us to erect barriers to this love. These barriers are our own personal sins.

(4) *plain old, undue pride*—a type of self-isolation and independence which results in a hiding of one's true self and a refusal to ask for help. This arises from the misconception that we must come to God first and do all the work ourselves. It keeps us from reaching out to others for help with relationships and other life problems. Such independence ultimately turns into isolation from others.

(5) *fear of the implications of this gift,* due to fear of God. Those of us who were taught to believe in a God who judges harshly, who is wrathful, who punishes, who is like a demanding mother or father, spouse, or employer have a hard time even wanting to become aware of God within. If God can hurt so intensely, we reason, then isn't it better to keep God at the greatest distance possible? We need—somehow—to first receive the awareness that the Selfhood of God is love and love alone, and that is the *only* thing that God is constantly gifting us with, constantly pouring into our minds, hearts, bodies, and souls, whether we realize it or not.

Dwelling Places of the Most High

The key to entrance into all honest, deeply-shared relationships with other people and all of creation is our willingness to enter into relationship with God. This gift of conscious, loving, reciprocal, oneness-in-presence with the God who dwells within us is "THE" gift. It is the essence, the overwhelming truth of what human existence is all about. It is a truth so radical that it is hard to fathom, even more difficult to accept. How can I (acutely aware of all my failures to love God and my brothers and sisters) possibly be a "dwelling place of the Most High?" we ask ourselves, tempted to disbelieve, to discredit this promise. But the awed awareness and acceptance of this freely-given and unearned gift for our own individual lives is the beginning of new life for us. It is the beginning of the transformation of our lives into the life of Christ. It is the awakening of a new vision of ourselves, of our relationships with others, of our connection with all of reality, and of our place in reality. This new vision is the vision and the experience of presence—the shared feeling and understanding of the Love that life is all about.

We are called to become increasingly aware that our place in reality is right smack in the center of God. Because of this gift—God's presence and our capacity for the awareness and sharing of this presence—we are invited and enabled to participate actively in the family life of the three Persons of the Trinity. Paul wrote, "You have been adopted into the very family circle of God and you can say with a full heart, 'Father, my Father.' The Spirit himself endorses our inward conviction that we really are the children of God" (Rom. 8:15-17, paraphrase by Kenneth Kinghorn, *Fresh Wind of the Spirit*).

The Family Life of the Trinity

This family life of the Trinity is a life of constant, dynamic, creative loving—loving of one another and all of creation. It is unending presence of one to another. It is truly a love affair of infinite dimensions, one which will only deepen and expand as we stretch to love more and more widely and selflessly. To go one step further, it is the fulfillment of Christ's promise that he would not leave us orphans, for it is an invitation to become aware that we are one of their beloved children, playing always in the lap of the Trinity. This, and nothing less, is the spiritual call of later life, the call to enter into the abundantly loving family life of the Trinity.

I realize that this whole concept of Trinity may sound old-fashioned, even archaic and unnecessary to you. You may not resonate at all with a theology that is based so strongly on the Trinity. We don't talk about the Godhead, the Three Persons, etc. as Trinity very much. It has never really been a very popular concept, mainly because in the early years of the development of this concept, theologians spent too much time trying to figure out the dynamics of how the Father, Son, and Spirit interact with one another within the Trinity itself. Who can possibly know that? All of that is pure speculation and is probably none of our business (except that, if one is really fascinated by God, *everything* is open to thought, speculation, and contemplation).

Christ is really the one who first told us about and continues to inform us about the Trinity. We cannot "know" the Trinity outside of Christ and what he tells us. He speaks of the Father and paints for us a picture of how the Father loves us and cares for us, even to the point of knowing every hair on our heads. Christ tells us about his own relationship with the Father when he calls God "Abba." Christ also tells us about the Spirit when he promises that we will not be left orphans. It is the Spirit who enables us to be in unity with the Trinity and with each other. It is as though we, all together as the family of humankind, complete the fullness of the Trinity in some mysterious and glorious way.

I've been "worrying" the Trinity as a dog worries its bone for a long time. When I was about five years old and unable to go to school for a year due to a bout with rheumatic fever, my mother taught me my school lessons at home. The "mystery" of the Trinity was one of the lessons. I couldn't understand it and became very frustrated. My mother brushed off that particular lesson, saying that it was a mystery and not to bother with it—no human being could ever understand it, nor was she expected to do so. I was incensed. Why would God create a mystery, tell everybody about it, then say "Ha, Ha, that's for me to know and you to find out!" (a common saying among kids when I was young).

I took it on as my special "think-project," and I've been ruminating about it ever since. Rather than being an irrelevant, esoteric waste of time, it has been the ongoing and deepening basis of my spirituality, my faith life. I think it is a magnificent conceptual framework for understanding how God interacts with us, too!

I invite you to open yourself to the fullness of the loving Trinity and to pray often our commonly sung doxology:

Praise God, from whom all blessings flow;
Praise him, all creatures here below;
Praise him above, ye heavenly host;
Praise Father, Son, and Holy Ghost.

7

❦

RECEIVING THE GIFT OF GIFTS

*For I tell you this; one loving blind desire for God alone is more
valuable in itself, more pleasing to God and to the saints, more
beneficial to your own growth, and more helpful to your friends,
both living and dead, than anything else you could do.*

The Cloud of Unknowing

CATHERINE'S STORY MAY BE TYPICAL OF THE OLDER ADULT
Christian, who finds herself in a state of emptiness, of "spiritual
dryness," as the old spiritual masters used to call it. Up to the point
when she came to see me about her depression she had led a good,
useful, and dedicated Christian life. This life was oriented to the
more external aspects of her religion—church attendance and
public worship, dutifully performed works of charity, organized
fellowship. She prayed, but her prayer was formal and intellectual;
it did not arise, living, from the depths of her heart.

This faithful woman truly loved God; her love was a product
of the discipline of her will. There is absolutely nothing "wrong"
with this state of being; it is a true life of faith. The only problem
was that she was missing out on something more, and she felt that
emptiness. She couldn't put her finger on what was wrong, and no
one else seemed to be able to help her. Certainly no new external
activity helped at all. It just made her emptiness worse.

What Catherine did not know was that God was inviting her
to enjoy a much more intimate relationship—calling her to an
indescribable immediacy and completeness of God's presence that

she didn't realize was available to her. She had not yet entered into an experienced, mutual love affair with her God. To Catherine, God was not present to her as an intimate, loving Presence, but was a distant, impersonal Reality existing in some other dimension, totally "other" rather than both other and personal. She was not even able to experience the tremendous awe of this "otherness." She believed intellectually the Gospels that taught her that God is Love, but she had never felt herself to be a participant in this Love. What was to be her next step? What is the next step for anyone in this spiritual state? How can God become an intimate reality for Catherine and for all of us who seek such intimacy? How can we experience God as being present to us—as the ultimate Presence of love?

Experiences of God's Presence

Think about a time in your early life when you felt you might have had an experience of God. Children often have experiences of this sort, but by the time they are ready for school they may have actually learned *not* to be able to feel God's presence. One of the most moving experiences I have witnessed happened to my godchild, Libby Eilers. Libby is the youngest of a family of three children; her brother Jody was eighteen and her sister Mayme twelve at the time. We—her parents, brother and sister, Ron and I, and two grandparents were celebrating Libby's fourth birthday. As is our custom I told Libby the story of the night she was born. (The very same group had been in attendance, waiting for her appearance.) Then her mother, Barbara, turned off all the lights and brought in the cake with the candles lit, ready to be blown out. Her sister and I were ready with the camera, waiting for the perfect moment. But Libby did not blow out her candles. We waited. Nothing happened. Finally her mother said, with some exasperation, "Libby, hurry up and blow out your candles!" Libby replied, clutching her arms around herself, "Wait, wait. I feel like God's having a party in my heart!" Needless to say, we waited.

I believe the experience that John Wesley had at Aldersgate was also an experience of God's presence. He claimed that his heart felt "strangely warmed." He was changed in some way; he became more confident of God's love for him because of the experience, which was certainly a significant one for him for the rest of his life. Thomas Merton had an unexpected experience of oneness with all of humanity while standing at the corner of Fourth and Walnut Streets in downtown Louisville, Kentucky, that changed his life. Of this experience Merton wrote:

> In Louisville, on the corner of Fourth and Walnut, in the center of the shopping district, I was suddenly overwhelmed with the realization that I loved all these people, that they were mine and I was theirs, that we could not be alien to one another, even though we were total strangers. . . . I have the immense joy of being human, a member of the race in which God himself became incarnate .ʾ . . as if the sorrows and stupidities of the human condition could overwhelm me—now that I realize what we really are.
>
> If only everybody could understand this! But it cannot be explained. There is no way of convincing people that they are walking around shining like the sun!

What are we supposed to do with an invitation like this—an invitation to experience God's presence, to live the family life of the Trinity? How do we prepare ourselves to respond to such an incredible gift?

Responding to the Invitation

Here are some formal steps we can take to facilitate our response. We are first invited to become **aware** of the reality of the presence of God within us. Do we really believe (but not necessarily feel or experience) the teachings of scripture—that the kingdom of God, that God's Self, is within us, that the Father as creativity, the Son as love, and the Spirit as the energy that marries them and then infuses love and creativity into the world dwell in us and that we are part of that life? If we can say even a hesitant yes to this question, even if all we can manage is the desire to believe, we are preparing ourselves to receive this gift.

Our next task is to accept the second part of the gift: we must **acknowledge** the fact that the awareness and experience of this presence is available to us if we desire it strongly enough. We must also be willing to share it with others, for we must be willing to become present to others, just as God is to us.

Next we must **ask** for this gift with great singleness of desire combined with hope, belief, and trust that it will be given because God wants to give knowledge and experience of this love to us.

Once we receive this gift (and it will be given, but in God's own time and dependent on our preparedness), we must **accept** it with an attitude of **appreciation, gratefulness**, and **inner poverty**. We must know that we have not earned this gift, nor can we give it to ourselves. Because it is pure gift, it flows from the generosity of the love of God for us.

Next, we must **nurture** this ever-deepening, ever-expanding, love relationship with the Father, Son, and Spirit within our hearts and in the hearts of our neighbors, for this love is given not just to us alone; it is meant always to flow through us and outward toward the world.

Finally, we must keep in mind that at some point we may be asked to **let go**, to relinquish our awareness and enjoyment of this relationship. Because the joys of this relationship can be so intense, especially for people who are gifted with a more emotional personality type, there can arise the temptation to love the fact of being in relationship more than concentrating purely and totally on the One whom we love. When we enjoy the relationship more than the Loved One, we are really focusing selfishly on ourselves and our feeling state. Believe it or not, we can even become greedy for the experience of relationship with God! The old masters call this "spiritual gluttony."

Only when we are willing and able to relinquish our need and desire for the enjoyment of relating to God will we have finally found ourselves hidden securely in Love Itself. Loving the relationship more than the Lover has its human counterpart. Have you ever known a person who was more enthusiastically caught up in all the details of her engagement parties and wedding plans than in the person whom she was marrying? It seems to me that this happens all too frequently, and it does not bode well for a successful marriage once the initial excitement dies down.

In addition, illnesses of various kinds can at times interfere with our ability to experience God. Severe depression and stroke can appear to "cut off" our sense of God's presence. At these times we will need to depend on our will to love and pure faith to believe that God still exists and loves us. This is difficult, but it is an immensely powerful force in the world. It is pleasing to God because it is selfless loving.

If such an intimate relationship with God seems like too enormous a gift to be bestowed on us, we need to recall, over and over again, as our innermost constant prayer, the words of Christ: "We shall come to him and make our home with him" (John 14:23).

Can you realize, even to the slightest degree, that the Trinity—the wholeness and completeness of God—the Father, Son, and Spirit—have sought you out as their home and are constantly present to you? That they are the source of creation, the principle of love that keeps creation expanding, and the energy which gives power and direction to love? That wherever you go, with whomever you are spending time, at each moment of the day and night, waking and sleeping, you bear the Triune God within you? That God does not dwell in some vague place but permeates your whole being; your mind, your soul? That every tiny cell of your body is vitally engaged in the family life of the Trinity? That they are calling you constantly into consciousness of their presence? That they are inviting you to enter into the union of their love, to become one with them in their intense love of one another and the created universe?

I think that if we allowed ourselves to become fully aware of this reality, of this awesome promise, and if we responded to it in trust by surrendering our whole selves to the truth of this gift, our lives would be transformed very quickly into the likeness of Christ here on earth. Our minds would become the compassionate mind of Christ. Our actions would be the healing actions of Christ. Our relationships would be the intimate sharing of Christ's relationships. Our body would be Christ's body. Our loving would be directed to the Father and to all the Father's children, past, present, and future. For the ultimate goal of our yearning and our reaching out for God's love in this life is to be able to say, as Paul said, "It is no longer I who live, but it is Christ who lives in me" (Gal. 2:20 NRSV). The purpose of our lives as lovers and followers of Christ is to become another Christ-gift to the world from its Creator.

What keeps you from a full realization of this promise of conscious union with God and its significance for your own life? Have you given it very much thought over the years? Do you doubt that you, a human being, are capable of knowing and experiencing God, or anything spiritual, for that matter? We value the rationality of our intellect to such a degree that we often kill anything that resembles an experience, a feeling, when it seems to relate to God or anything that smacks of the transcendent. Most of us are really afraid of having an experience of God. Yet, one of the most fascinating pieces of information that I have come across in a long time points to possible scientific evidence for our physiological capacity to experience God. (I must say that I have not examined the formal research analysis which forms the basis of this study.) In his book, *Closer to the Light,* pediatrician Melvin Morse discusses the results of ten years of research on near-death experiences of children. He states:

> Our research brought together new and preexisting information that revealed a genetically imprinted circuit in the brain that can generate the near-death experience. The existence of that area has caused me to include the concept of the soul in my medical thinking. I have documented that we have an area in the brain, the right temporal lobe, that some researchers describe as the seat of the soul. It is connected to the hippocampus, which serves as the brain's master control, sorting out thousands of pieces of sensory input and deciding which of them should be acted upon. . . .
> The hippocampus has been called the "man in the machine" by some neurologists. It is directly connected to areas in the right

temporal and occipital lobes that contain the neuronal circuitry to create near-death experiences. The collapse of the visual fields to create the tunnel experience occurs in the occipital lobes. The sensations of leaving the body, seeing dead relatives, hearing heavenly music, speaking with God, and reviewing one's own life are part of our genetic makeup, "hard-wired" into each of us.

Near-death experiences are an example of a psychological experience that can be anatomically located within the brain. Since they are often profound and mystical experiences, the study of NDEs [near death experiences] will help to reunite the centuries-old split of science and spirit. I once heard a minister preach that a small piece of God is in each and every one of us. I thought to myself: "God is in each and every one of us, and the ability to perceive God is located in the right temporal lobe, within the Sylvian fissure."

If the above research has any validity at all, God has programmed you physiologically from birth to be able to be in a union of continual, loving communication with God. God is constantly pouring out the energy of love into your own personhood—your body and mind and relationships and work and creative activities and hurts—all that is you. The only problem is that if you are not aware of this, you are apt to have a difficult time responding in a way that will enable your relationship with God to grow. It's like having a television and not knowing that you have to plug it in, in order for it to work and bring you your favorite program.

I invite you, for the rest of the time you spend with this book, to let yourself be enveloped by the gift of God's Self to you. Let the truth of God's indwelling presence sweep over you and gather you into itself. Remember yourself as you were when you were a child, then picture yourself held and cuddled in the arms of God.

Becoming Aware of the Trinity

If the idea of the Trinity of creative love-energy dwelling with you is a bit overwhelming and too abstract, spend some time today just pondering the concept of Trinity and the energy that is released by the three Persons loving one another and all of creation, which includes you. Let yourself be assured that if you want this consciousness of the indwelling presence, God will enable you to become aware of and to experience this love. God wants your awareness and has created you to be able to experience this presence. Again—only if you want to. God is not above luring you into this relationship, but God will not violate your freedom to choose. If you desire it, you must actively and wholeheartedly ask for such awareness, and you must be ready to say yes when it is offered.

Here are some "awareness" techniques that you might use just to heighten your consciousness of the functions and presence of the three persons of the Trinity. They will sound very silly—to the point of being bizarre—and not religious or spiritual at all. But they are part of our daily experience, and this is what we're trying to do—become aware of God in all things. After a while they will act as "triggers" to an awareness of God in things you would not previously have connected with God. For a while these triggers will help you sustain an intellectual awareness of Trinity—a visual concept. Sooner or later this concept will no longer be needed and will drop away.

1. *Look for the number three.* It's everywhere—on auto license plates, bank statements, grocery prices, ZIP codes, telephone numbers.

2. *Look for triangles.* They're slightly harder to find, but you'll see them if you look. I happen to like to wear triangular earrings, a simple and hidden reminder to myself of my own relationship with the three Persons. (Don't worry that someone will think you are strange. I can assure you that no one to date has ever come up to me and said, "Oh, I see you're wearing a symbol of the Trinity. How nice! Where can I get a pair of those?")

You might also like to look for triangular stones and rocks. Whenever I am walking in the park or at the lake, I am on the watch for particularly well-formed triangular rocks. I have an interesting collection of them. When I keep a small one in my pocket, I can return to it over and over; it serves as a reminder of God in creation; it "grounds me" in God's presence.

3. Listen for the number three. It is in conversation, on radio, on television.

4. Most important, memorize John 14:23:"We shall come to him and make our home with him." Repeat this over and over, as often as you can, during the day. Say it as slowly as you can, trying to absorb the meaning for you. If you have trouble memorizing it, write it down and keep it with you so that you can read it often. Ask God to allow you to see the full significance of those words.

You may find these activities exceedingly strange, but this is merely a sensitization exercise. It is designed to heighten your consciousness to enable you to become tuned into the idea of the Trinity by using everyday, material reality that is not normally connected with spiritual reality, as sign and symbol. In our Christian upbringing we don't concentrate very much on Trinity, the idea of the Father/Creator-Mother, Son/Lover-Teacher, and Spirit/Energizer-Guide loving each other and the world together in dynamic tandem. We think mostly of the Father and Christ, and occasionally the Spirit, and we keep them separate. We don't look at the functions or work of the members of the Trinity. Many of us have a favorite Person we relate to most often, in a specific context. We may focus our attention on the crucified Christ. An image of the cross helps us to keep this in mind. We think of the Father as Creator, who goes mostly image-less except for those pictures that portray him as a bearded old man. The Spirit is imaged as dove or flame. There are lots of dove-pins and crosses around, but not many symbols of the Trinity.

Again, the idea of Trinity may seem to be just too difficult, esoteric, and awesome for us to contemplate. The temptation is to leave it for the theologians to chew on. However, when we relinquish contemplation of the Trinity to the experts, we are giving up the possibility of experiencing the wholeness of our Christian faith in the fullness of its mature functioning. We need to be creators and lovers. We need the energy of the Spirit to help cocreate love in this world. We need to keep in mind always that when we are in full, conscious participation with the Trinity we are empowered to become the creative fingertips of God, the creative lovers of the world in this time and in this place.

Feel free to play with and develop your own concept of the Trinity. Can you create a mental image of the three persons interacting among themselves and with you? Who is the Creator to you—father, mother, artist? inventor? judge? Who is Christ—brother, friend, lover, acquaintance, employer? Who is the Spirit to you—energy, power, wisdom, giver of gifts, advocate? There are no right or wrong images—what comes to you tells you something about who you are, what you value, and what your experiences have been; it is for your own benefit; it may change as your relationship with the Trinity changes.

I love science, especially physiology and physics. In my own mind I sometimes compare the members of the Trinity to the three major parts of the atom—the proton, electron, and neutron, all of which need to be working together in dynamic tension in order for energy to be emitted for use in the world. At other times this image is far too scientific and impersonal, and I can't relate to it at all, and must imagine a family scene. Most of the time there is no mental image at all, and that's fine, too. The important thing is that you take the time to ponder the mystery of the Trinity in your own life; however you do that is unique and special to you.

Deciding to Accept the Gift

Stop and consider your own experience once again.

How aware are you of the presence of God within you as well as all around you? How do you *feel* about this idea of the Father, Son, and Spirit making their home within you? Are you frightened? Does the idea evoke joy? Dread? Anxiety? Disbelief? No response at all?

More than likely, at first you will have no response at all, or you will be attempting to dredge up some appropriately religious sentiment in response to this question. Don't do that. Instead, let's take a look at the psycho-spiritual steps we can take to prepare ourselves to receive the gift of the awareness of the presence of God the Father, Son, and Spirit within us.

First of all, you must *decide* whether or not you really want the gift of this consciousness, this awareness of the presence of the Father, Son, and Spirit within. At first consideration such consciousness seems to be an appropriate thing for a Christian to want to experience, the next step on your lifelong spiritual journey, and you might as well "go for it." But this awareness of presence is not just another challenge to be added to the complexity of life, another goal to be sought, another task to be mastered. This is radically different. It is the abundance of life, the fullness of being which is offered, but not without cost.

The development of the ability to receive this gift does not come automatically, without effort, although this effort is truly, in the words of my husband, Ron, a "wonderful chore." It requires that you allow yourself to become present in and to your own life. This means that you become present to God, to yourself, and to other people simultaneously. It also requires that you respond with a "yes" to the expansion and intensification of loving presence in your life—your inner life with yourself and your outer life with other people. It will ultimately require the total gift in return of your own self—body, mind, and soul—back to God to be transformed and used in whatever way God sees fit to enable you to work for the well-being of the universe and all that is in it.

What does this mean to you in terms of real life? It means that you must develop some skills that will enable you to live in the present. It is only by being able to experience the present that any of us can experience Presence. It means developing skills that will open you to the presence of God, such as meditative or "being with" prayer. It means becoming present to yourself by taking a long, hard, honest look at the early, maladaptive learnings and the deliberate sins that keep you from knowing who you really are inside. It means learning new, loving behaviors. It means learning how to be present to other people on a more honest and deep level. It means learning to know who you are and how to share with others who you really are in the eyes of God. It means inviting others to share who they are with you.

Not an easy task, by any stretch of the imagination. But it *is* what we are all here for. And it does lead to life in the kingdom of God. On earth. Before death. Amazing!

What will happen if you choose to open yourself to this abundance of life? What will happen to you if you open your consciousness to the awareness of God's presence within and around you and to the oneness with God which is offered you?

Christ, the prophets, the evangelists, the disciples, the martyrs, the hermits, the fathers and mothers of the church, the founders, the reformers, the mystics—all of those individuals who have been intensely involved with God throughout the ages—tell us, through the example of their lives and through their writings, a similar story.

Experiencing Love's Embrace

They say that when you say yes, when you open yourself to Loving Presence—the presence of God, yourself, and other people—with your whole heart and mind and soul and body, you will fall in Love. In love with Love. Because Love lives in you and embraces you and has been pouring love unceasingly into your entire being from the moment of your conception. And while you were being knitted in your mother's womb. And on the day of your birth. And at the moment of your first awareness of your own self.

From the first second of your existence, Love has been overflowing into you, growing you, mothering you, fathering you. Delighting in you. Never taking loving eyes away from you, whatever you did, however you behaved. And Love will continue this embrace into eternity.

Love lives not only in you but in the persons next to you and in humanity half a globe away. Love brings you all together to create a single harmony, playing Its own love song from the depths of your innermost cells to the farthest reaches of the universe.

So—all at once or little by little—you will fall in love with the God who first loved you. This experience of falling in love with God can take as many forms as there are people for God to love, simply because we are all unique creations and, as such, are loved uniquely. You actually may be surprised both at the way in which this love manifests itself in your life and at the way in which you respond. For example, you may ordinarily be the unsentimental, "rational" type yet experience your relationship with God as a truly romantic, passionate love affair. Or, you may find yourself involved in the deepest, most caring, quiet, and comforting friendship you have ever known. You may be overwhelmed by the grandeur of the creator God who encompasses the entire cosmos, the God who cannot be constrained by a name or an image, or even an idea, yet exists in all that is. Or, God may be your challenging mentor, the one with whom you wrestle and become angry, the one from whom you try to flee, the irresistible one who goads you—oftentimes against your will—into becoming who you really are. God may be the silent "ground" of your existence, the still point of your being, the one who sleeps in the boat of your soul. And God may even be your mother—the one who nurtures you and teaches you to nurse all of creation. You may know only the absence of God—the sense of absence that is so intense that it permeates your entire life with longing for the only thing that you are capable of desiring.

These are just a few of the ways of relating to God. Be aware that there is no "good," "better," or "best" way to be in relationship with God—the important thing is for you to allow yourself to grow in conscious relationship. You may even experience different ways of being in relationship with God at different times of your life (even at different times of the day!), depending on your immediate need, your life situation, your physical health and emotional state, and the needs of the people in your life. Psychiatrist Gerald May in *The Awakened Heart* advises, "If you seek a way of relating to God, you can do no better than to let God come into your awareness as God will. Be open to any possibilities, willing to be surprised."

However you experience this relationship with Love, with your yes to a deeper involvement you will have taken the first step into the awareness that you really are now, and always have been, in constant union with God. *You have never been separated.* The sense of separation is an illusion which comes from early—and necessary, to a certain degree—weaning away from the truth of our unity with God, mother, and others; for we do need to become independent persons. The problem lies in the fact that we are led to the other extreme of independence, which creates the illusion of aloneness, of separateness, of orphanhood. We could just as easily have been taught to relate to the loving God within us as we were taught to honor the God who lives somewhere in Heaven. We could just as easily have been taught brother/sisterhood as we were taught to compete with one another in a pervasive atmosphere of greed.

In addition, along with the growing realization of union comes the awareness that you are living now in the reality, the kingdom of God, which is your own true home, the home you share with all others and all of creation.

So you will fall in Love. In love with Love. In love with all that is loved.

Totally. Infinitely. Irrevocably. Head-over-heels in Love.

What Will Happen Next?

If you say yes to this invitation to love in whatever ways Love manifests Love's Self to you, you will enter into an affair of the soul which will continue all the days of your life. It will awaken you and enliven you to the loving presence of God and all of God's creation. You will join with others throughout the ages on a journey both inward and outward, to "the still point of the turning world" as T. S. Eliot puts it, the place of unity where all things, all persons, all meanings converge and rest in contemplative appreciation and enjoyment of each other. Because God's Self is manifested so uniquely in every person, this journey will be different for each human being, yet it has a direction that is common to most people who respond to the love of God for them.

Two people whose whole lives were devoted to living in the presence of God, Teresa of Avila and John of the Cross, described in great detail the psycho-spiritual process of coming to awareness of one's union with God in Love. Both of them lived in Spain in the sixteenth century and reformed their Carmelite order of nuns and friars. In general, according to them and many others who have yearned to "dwell in the house of the Lord all the days of their lives," the journey into the full awareness of Love may be described in this way:

Your constantly-expanding awareness of the gift of God's Self to you will become increasingly attractive and will draw you into the Love of the three Persons ever more deeply as each day goes by. You will be given the knowledge and experience of being loved more completely than you have ever been loved before. You may even realize that you have never been truly loved before in your entire life. Nor have you been able to love others or even recognize and enjoy the love they offer you because of the lack of nurture you experienced at various times in your own life, especially in the early years. God's love will help you to heal the empty, dark, and sad places in your mind and soul that result from not having been loved as a child or as an adult.

This love of God for you will become irresistible, and you will follow it almost effortlessly wherever it leads you. It will guide you to lovely places in your own soul and in the souls of others. You will become strengthened in this Love, and your own ability to return love will deepen and expand.

Eventually, at some point that can never be predicted or planned, you will find yourself called into the deep and vast solitude of your own soul where God will speak to your heart. There God will gently tell you how you need to grow, what you need to do (or not do), how you need to be, how you can respond in order to prepare yourself to deepen your awareness of love and to receive even more love. God's voice will be understood by you in whatever way you learn best—through people, events, reading, places, inner promptings, intuitions, feelings. What God communicates to you always calls you to expand, to go beyond both the comfortable and the painful limits you have set for yourself. God is now inviting you to become more of who you *really* are.

At this point you may be tempted to go back to the predictable ordinariness of your old, "normal," more comfortable way of being with God, of keeping God at a safe and proper distance. But you will discover that, deep down, you no longer really want such superficiality. You will find that once you have tasted God, no other food will suffice. Desire for the full awareness of your oneness with God will become your chronic and lovely ache, your constant yearning. Even in times of tiredness and burden and challenge and distaste for things spiritual, when you try to get rid of this knowledge of God that you have been given, with whatever means you choose to distract yourself, you will never again be fully satisfied by anything else.

If you allow yourself to experience it and to trust it, this growing desire, this awe-full ache for God will lead you more and more fully into the energy-giving family love of the Father, the Father's Son, and their Spirit. Almost without noticing you will find yourself surprised by what you are becoming, for without even trying—perhaps without even being conscious of it—you will find yourself responding to their life. Your response will cause you to change, as you grow more and more attuned to the movement and life of the Spirit within and around you. You will become increasingly aware of the ways in which you have difficulty loving and why, and you will be taught patiently again and again how to love and how to be loved. God never tires of scooping you up in times of failure or discouragement, brushing you off, and setting you on your feet again—that is God's immense delight! You will find that this inner life with God becomes your centerpoint, the basis from which your whole life flows. Sooner or later, you will know that it *is* your life. You will find yourself singing, as did the Beloved in the Song of Solomon, "I am my Beloved's, and my Beloved is mine" (The Song of Songs 6:2).

Not for You Alone

But this lovely ache for God, while seeming very intimate and very private, is not a gift for you alone. It is not your individual road to salvation. It is not your personal source of joy and peace, love and consolation, your "private stock" of happiness. For it is not just your own inner self that is affected by your desire for God. On the contrary, this ache will, in time, become so expansive in you that it will not be able to be contained within the narrow confines of your own mind and body. It will want to become public, for it belongs to the entire body of Christ. Because it is held in common with the whole body of Christ, you will be given the desire to witness to it, to express it in some kind of action. This action lies on a continuum from deep, contemplative, hidden, "being with" prayer to politics because it is meant for others as much as it is for you. God gives the awareness of this loving presence to those who will accept and nurture it so that they can share this love with the rest of the world. So be confident that sooner or later, when God (not you) knows you are ready, you will be invited and privileged to express this love or witness to it in some way unique to you and corresponding with your other gifts.

Eventually who, what, where, and how you are given the opportunity to love may not coincide exactly with who, what, where, and how you want or have chosen to love. You may experience some conflict between what has become easy for you and what you feel you are being invited to do. You have already responded with yes to God's love. But on this journey there is always more love to open up to, there are ever-increasing gifts to receive, there is always an expanding boundary of interest and deep concern when you love. For example, if you limit yourself to the love of your own faith community one day, you may be invited to add the love of a new and perhaps different community the next. You are called quietly and constantly to stretch beyond the comfortable to reach for your own freedom and to help others do the same. But because there is always so much to distract you from yourself in the everyday, external world, God will constantly draw you within your soul and will speak to your heart.

Here God will lovingly reveal to you a few more of the barriers that exist within you, barriers which impede your receiving the full awareness of the love that God is constantly pouring into your heart and wants to pour into the world through you. You yourself will be free to decide if and how you want to relinquish these barriers; God will never coerce you into giving them up. If you open yourself to knowledge of them, the full realization of these barriers may block for a time your awareness of the closeness of God, due to feelings of shame or remorse that you may experience. You may even be tempted to say that you are not worthy of this intimate life with God. But disregard these temptations—God does not want you to waste a single second wallowing in any feelings that separate you from this love.

One of the barriers common to many people on this path, which you may share with them, is a limited idea of who God is. You may be stuck in a relationship with God that is based on an image that is outdated, childish, or even unhealthy for your stage of psychological and spiritual development. You are invited to expand this image or concept of God that no longer works for you. Because God cannot be contained in a mental image or concept, you are invited to examine all of your own ideas of God, to see if they benefit you. For example, you may image God as a father, yet you may have created him in the image of your own, human father, who may have punished you or judged you more than he was able to demonstrate his love for you. This old image that you impose on God will no longer be helpful to you as you mature. In the process of outgrowing a narrow image of God, you may experience a time when you have no idea at all who or what or if God is. For a while, you may feel abandoned by God. But you have not been abandoned. God is with you, even if you can't realize it.

Gradually, you may come to realize that you are able to experience more and more freedom to play with who God is. As you shed images of God that are not really God, you become free to relate to the God *who is.*

The awareness of your barriers to love, and the surrender of your former, more comfortable image of a separate, well-defined God may be difficult for you for a while. Before you fell in love with God, you thought you were a reasonably good person; you thought you had a handle on things. God had a specific place in your life and you thought you were doing the work of your God.

And you were—a good person doing *your* idea of work for your definition of God within the limits of your own human activity. But now you are being invited to go vast distances beyond that. You are being invited to relinquish your own limited ideas about who God is and what God does so that you, too, can become a lover of creation and of the family of humankind, just as Christ is. You are being invited to join in partnership with God so that God can be free to act with you and in you without constraint, in the service of Love. You are being invited to allow Christ's gift to the world to be your gift to the world. You are to be "about your Father's business." Your vocation, for as long as you are on this earth, and perhaps even afterwards, until the final resurrection, is to become a Christ-gift to the world. The only boundary to your loving is to be the outer boundary of the known universe. God alone can be depended upon to take your love beyond the known boundary into the realm of the "communion of saints."

I like to imagine this "communion of saints" to be all those lovers of God who completed their earth-lives before us and who are still with us in some spiritual way. I like to think that they are now nurturing, maternal souls who help us help God to bring the kingdom into being, and whose work it is to help us become more and more responsive to Love. Somehow it is very comforting to think that the whole communion of saints is cheering us on! I know many widows and widowers and bereaved parents who think of their loved ones in this way, and are extraordinarily nurtured not just by their memory, but by a confidence that they are still actively helping them and interested in their lives.

A New Vocation

Back to vocation. When and if you say yes to this further invitation to full awareness of your union with the Trinity, you will joyfully begin your journey to the cross. You will commence your final dying process, dying to all that remains within your self that clouds your consciousness of the presence of God. You will become a Christ-gift to other people, as the love of God surges continually through you to them. In your giving you will never be depleted, for you will be like a cup of water which, when filled beyond its brim, overflows in all directions steadily, constantly, and peacefully. Thus, you will become an ever more perfect giver of the Father's gifts to his children.

God, delightedly taking your yes to be total and unequivocal, will quickly and lovingly show you the most entrenched, difficult, and often the most subtle barriers that are in the way of your awareness of love. These barriers are often actually spiritual ones! Perhaps they are attachment to the comfort and joy of particular ways of praying or the satisfaction of serving others in some way that you greatly enjoy.

I remember one elderly Baptist man who came for counseling. He was very depressed and had lost all meaning in his life. It seems that he'd been just fine, involved in many dearly-loved church activities, especially active driving the church bus to all kinds of events. When he turned eighty-five and it was obvious that he was having difficulty turning his head, due to arthritis of the neck, the pastor asked him not to continue driving. However, he did not suggest an alternative activity that fit my patient's self-image. During the process of counseling, he took a long, hard, and often painful look at his attachment to the bus-driving and realized (not too enthusiastically at first) that God might be calling him to do something different with his talents. He and his wife finally decided to reach out beyond their own boundaries to some refugees who had been resettled in their neighborhood. They learned how to teach English as a second language and are both now enthusiastic supporters of the people they work with, who are of an entirely different culture. My patient, by giving up his former attachment to a "good," expanded beyond his limits into new, exciting realms of loving activity. He and his wife are models of how people can change and grow in late life and are an inspiration to the entire community.

This process of outgrowing and then relinquishing barriers that were actually good for you at one time in your life may be experienced in your innermost being as a strange mixture of both intense suffering and great joy. You may feel disconnected from your "old" self. Sort of disjointed, out of sorts. Out of contact with who you have known yourself to be. At your deepest level you trust that you will be gathered back, realigned, fixed, then put back together in a different form, but you don't know when, or how, or if you will even recognize who you have become.

Feeling God's Absence

For a little while you may think you have lost contact with God (like the astronauts who lose contact with Earth when they travel to the dark side of the moon). You may not only feel that God has abandoned you, but you might be tempted to believe that God does not even exist. You may think this whole thing has been a figment of your imagination. You may be very angry and feel that you have been duped, seduced, led into nothingness. Your only prayer (if you have any ability to pray) may be a groaning in the dark, "Out of the depths I cry to you O Lord. Lord, hear my prayer," and "My God, my God, why have you forsaken me?"

This experience of God's absence occurs because even the healthy, mature image of God that you had created earlier on the path was not totally real, was not big enough, was not all that is. The God who is now becoming present to you, in you, with you— the God of your own identity—is the God of the All. This is the *God Who Is,* for all things, for all people, for all time, and for after time. This God of Love is awesome, because this God cannot be contained in any image, any concept known to humankind. The only way you can come to oneness with this God is through your relationship with the Son, Christ.

So you must cling with all your strength and singleness of mind at this time to Christ, confident that you are in the process of becoming an adopted child, so that you will be able, with and through Christ, to enter into the presence and to call the Father *Abba.* (A friend recently told me that her young grandson has informed her that he plans to get to heaven by sitting on Jesus' foot, winding his legs and arms around Christ's leg, and perching there while Christ walks around. He is confident that Christ will walk him right into heaven whenever he feels like it. What a perfect image for those of us at this stage!)

A New Place of Peace

When this process of dying to all within you that is not God has run its course and come to its proper end (all in God's time, in years or months or weeks or days or minutes and totally unpredictable and out of anyone's control to schedule), your true life will begin. This is the beginning of your "real" life because this is the life you were meant to live all along, the abundant life to which Jesus called you. There is no end point to the expansion of this life of love, no limit to its deepening and intensification. Keep in mind that because you are a human being, interacting with yourself and others in new situations all the time, you *will* inevitably construct new barriers to love. In other words, you will continue to sin in one way or another. But be confident that God will always very quickly scoop you up, help you to tear down the new barriers, brush you off, and bring you to a place of even deeper trust in the Love that is constantly drawing you back and deeper into Itself. This process of scooping you up and bringing you back home is God's delight. There is no trace of anger, wrath, or judgment in this prodigal love of God for you. God just delights in your desire to come back home.

In this state you will burn as a "living flame of love" for your God. You will be brought to a place of peace that is beyond anything you could have possibly imagined. You will feel wonderfully free and safe. You will experience not just your separate self and God's self, but a new, interactive yet mutual oneness, a living unity of compassion, concern, and love for all that exists. You will have become a full member of Christ's body here on earth. You will love as God loves, because you and God, in union that is conscious to you, will love together. Through you and in you and with you God will be able to be present to all people, to all of creation.

Most likely, you won't experience yourself doing this much "theologizing" or thinking about God, your response to God, or even your relationship with God. Rather, you will find that you have become free of the self-reflection that was characteristic of the earlier parts of your journey. Your vision will, once again, go outward, but in an entirely different way. You will not gaze outward in greed, attempting to grasp what you see, to bring it into permanent residence in you. Instead, you will look outward upon the world with the loving, giving eyes of Love so that Love will flow outward from you towards *everything* and *everyone* you see. This will happen automatically, without your even trying.

An example of this loss of self-reflection is Anna, a very elderly woman who explained her way of "being with" God to me and how it had changed over the years. She said, "I really don't think about God very much anymore, even though I used to. In the past my spiritual life was very complicated. I was always wondering if I were pleasing God, always concerned that I wasn't doing God's will "just right." Always thinking that I was not quite good enough. As I look back on it now, I realize that what was important to me was how *I* was *performing* for God. The emphasis was really always on me and what I was doing, even though I thought it was on God.

"Now, in my very old age, I've given up all of that performing stuff—probably because I don't have the energy for it any longer. I can't do much any more and I can't even think much, either. I forget a great deal. Now all I can do is look out at my little world—my house and cats and my dog and the people I hear about in other countries and the people who bathe me and bring me food and the sky and *everything,* and I just spend my time loving them. I just look at it all and I love it. Even though my eyesight is bad, in my mind's eye I see everything. It is all so very beautiful, even the bad things somehow get washed in the beauty of everything. I am so grateful for it all, grateful for *all* of my life, for all of life. Am I neglecting God because I don't think about him or talk to him anymore? I don't think so. Somehow, I feel that my looking and loving is enough for God—that that's all God ever really wanted from me in the first place—to love what he gave me. Don't you think so?"

What I think is that Anna's story is truly what the journey to God is all about. And it is very simple and utterly glorious at the same time.

Christ himself promised us this kind of relationship with God and one another in his prayer to the Father for us:

> May they all be one.
> Father, may they be one in us,
> as you are in me and I am in you,
> so that the world may believe it was you who sent me.
> I have given them the glory you gave to me,
> that they may be one as we are one.
> With me in them and you in me,
> may they be so completely one
> that the world will realise that it was you who sent me
> and that you have loved them as much as you loved me.
>
> John 17:21-23

Reaching Out to Others

Now, minute by minute, knowing that you are filled with love that is overflowing, God will put in your presence those who desperately need to be loved by God through you. They will come at all hours of the day and night, in many ways and shapes and forms—in actual physical presence or deep within your heart. They will not respect your desire for peace and quiet, your fear that you are "too old," or your excuse that you have already "done your part." They will come, expecting something from you, knowing not what. Your task will be to love them, in whatever way they need to be loved. Trust that you will be given everything you require to enable you to respond to their need for love. You must still be careful never to forget that your ego, your small "self" is not doing the loving. You are in Love and have yourself become the means through which Love can find its appropriate end. This is God's work and not your own project. Yours is the magnificent privilege of being invited to partnership in this work.

So this is truly the work of God that you are doing. This is Love working in you, with you, through you, as the essence of you—filling the world with wisdom and beauty, delight and compassion. This work is no mere pastime. Whatever you have done earlier, this is the most important work of all, even if it is small and hidden, even if no one else on earth knows about it. It is even better for being small and hidden, unknown to anyone but you and God. It may even be that you never become aware of the actual way in which you are being an instrumental part of God's love. This may be kept hidden from you. The important thing is that you have accepted your Loved One's invitation to love in this way. Have confidence that in the creative efficiency of God you will always be magnificently well employed.

Be aware also that the gift of this "work" of loving may cost you dearly, at some time and in some place, because the world of greed, the world that does not trust that it will be gifted with everything it needs, the world that refuses to believe it is living now in the kingdom of God, feels affronted by such love. It does not want to hear of it, to see it, to be reminded of it. And that is just what you do—you allow love to stay alive in the world; you help to bring the world back to Love itself. Again, this is not a mere pastime or a hobby, even if it is not your official role in the world. It is serious work; in some mysterious way the fate of the world may depend on your participation with others of Christ's body in this work. Perhaps it was for the sake of this work that God created you. The success of this work will never depend on what you perceive yourself to accomplish, for "successful," observable results can often be a deceptive smoke screen, and actually swerve you off course. Outwardly, you may look to the world like a fool or a failure. Be confident that this is no indication of the quality of your love.

In Bernanos' *Dialogues des Carmelites* a terrified Blanche, who is about to be guillotined because she will not renounce her faith, says to a perpetually and tiresomely jovial nun in her community, "Have you no fear that God may not tire of so much good humor, and may not come to you one day and say to you, as to Blessed Angela of Foligno: 'It was not for jesting that I loved thee'?"

For the Life of the World

This work, this "yes" to Love, is not for jesting at all. It is for the life of the world. It is the labor pains in the birthing of the kingdom. It may include generous measures of jesting and pleasure and joy. But it remains the means by which God's kingdom will come to fruition on earth. And until the kingdom is here completely, it is not for the purpose of jesting that we are being invited to do this work. It is for loving.

The author of the *Cloud of Unknowing* says of this work:

> All of mankind living on earth will be helped by this work in wonderful ways of which [we] are not even aware. . . For this is a work . . . that man would have continued to do if he had never sinned. And it was for this work that man was made, as all things also were made to help him and further him in this work, so that by means of it man shall be made whole again.

Please keep in mind that, while this journey into the life of Love may seem to be reserved for "special" people, and only rarely at that, it is meant for *every* Christian. We are *all* invited to this banquet, to this depth of relationship with God and with each other. We are *all* called to do this work. It is the abundant life. It is the realm, the kingdom of God on earth. It is the function, the maturation, of the Christian life. The only person who is excluded from this union of love is the person who chooses to exclude himself or herself. God's outpouring of love is constant and has been so since the beginning of time. We are the fickle ones.

And so we must choose; we must decide what it is that we truly want. Can we say, with the psalmist: "One thing I asked of the Lord . . . to live in the house of the Lord all the days of my life" (Psalm 127:4 NRSV)?

8

❦

THE MATURE SOUL

Every struggle that we make to live is a prayer to God for life. And the continuance of our existence is God's answer to our prayer. But when we first take the life which He gives us we do not know what it is. Its depth, its richness only opens to us gradually. Only gradually do we learn that God has given to us not merely the power of present being and present enjoyment, but that wrapt up and hidden in that He has given us the power of thinking, feeling, loving, living in such deep and lofty ways that we may be in connection with the great continuous unbroken thoughts and feelings and movements of the universe.

Phillips Brooks, *Sermons*

IF YOU FEEL, DEEP WITHIN YOUR HEART, SOME DEGREE of yearning for the kind of life with God that I have described; if, in your mind this radical invitation to transformation of life seems to be true to where God is leading you, your first step in response, as discussed in the previous chapter, was to **decide** that you want to follow this invitation. The next step is to **ask** for it. You must ask, for the life of conscious awareness of and oneness with the presence of God will not be imposed on you. God lures, invites, and beckons, but always waits for response before taking the next step. The initial response is up to you.

It may seem that what I have described is more of a challenge to your late life than you ever even wanted to know about, let alone take up. The description of the deepening love affair of the soul with God was not meant to frighten you away or to discourage you. However, you do need to know what such a commitment to Love's work involves, so that your decision will be made with some degree of awareness of the implications.

The implications are the same as they were for Jesus, when he decided to say yes to his life of total awareness of his identity with the Creator whom he called Father. This relationship with God is not to be embraced and entered into lightly, for it is strenuous and all-consuming and infinitely meaningful and extraordinarily important work that inevitably includes the cross and death to the self. Yet, I grow stronger daily in my belief that older adults, of all people, are best equipped psychologically and spiritually to enter these realms and to heed this spiritual call, this invitation to Presence. (Didn't Art Linkletter write a book called *Old Age Is Not for Sissies?*)

Well-Prepared for the Gift

Even though you may feel overwhelmed, too old, or perhaps not quite ready to respond to this spiritual invitation to conscious awareness of your oneness with God, be confident that you really have been well-prepared to receive this gift. Each day of your life has prepared you for this vocation. This is the first time in the history of humankind that there are so many people over the age of sixty-five. Why? At this stage in the history of humankind you are called to be another Abraham, a new Sarah. The world, which is so afraid of the aging process, needs you to model—define, demonstrate, and preach—the meaningfulness of later life. It has never been done before. You are to be prophet in this time. Take time right now to reread Genesis 17 and 18, which begins:

> When Abram was ninety-nine years old Yahweh appeared to him and said, "I am El Shaddai. Bear yourself blameless in my presence, and I will make a Covenant between myself and you, and increase your numbers greatly."
> Abram bowed to the ground. . . .
> Genesis 17:1-3

"As for Sarai your wife, you shall not call her Sarai, but Sarah. I will bless her and moreover give you a son by her. I will bless her and nations shall come out of her; kings of peoples shall descend from her."

Genesis 17:15-16

A new, world-changing project entrusted to a ninety-nine-year-old and an eighty-nine-year-old? A project that involved sex, pregnancy, childbirth, child-rearing, and the building of nations—pursuits we think of as belonging solely to the young and restless! What was God thinking of? Either God was crazy, desperate, or must like the elderly. Maybe *like* is the wrong word. God must think the elderly are the most competent, willing, and open people to be entrusted with such a significant mission. Old Abe and Sarah may not really have been that old, but they were certainly "past their prime." What do you think about their new calling?

What is to be your new vocation?

Are you ready to listen for it and to hear it?

As an older person and a mature follower of the teachings of Christ you have been strengthened and nurtured through the events of your entire lifetime for this work of living in the presence of God in many ways, day by day. Let's look at some of the ways in which the ground of your soul has been made fertile for this work and why you may be even better suited for the these tasks of Presence than a younger person might be:

♦ You have been given gifts throughout your lifetime to enjoy and develop and use, yet you have had to learn to relinquish them when asked to in order to grow into readiness for the next ones God has wanted to give you. So you know well the soul-wrenching yet purifying experience of having to make meaning of unexpected, involuntary loss.

♦ You also have had to learn to voluntarily let go of people, plans, places, things, and activities that were important and enjoyable to you. In your natural and very human resistance to these losses you have come face to face with the darkness that is greed in your own soul. You may still struggle with

99

attachment to these things, but you have noticed that as the years advance, it becomes easier and easier for you to relinquish them when it is necessary for you to do so.

◆ You know well the names of those whom you have refused to love, through neglect or deliberate intent, and you bear the burden of this refusal. You bear also the memoried wounds of those who have refused to love you for the same reasons. You accept your responsibility for your lack of love, and you forgive yourself. You do not accept undue responsibility for not having been adequately loved; you are, however, able to forgive those who should have loved you but did or could not.

◆ You have learned to recognize the limits of your small but over-inflated ego, because you have been battered again and again throughout the years by the results of your own self-centeredness. You have also learned to be gentle with yourself when your ego demands attention and acts out unattractively.

◆ You are familiar with the limits of your body and have come to the realization that while you live in your body and it is integral to you, it is not the essence of who you are. You are daily being reminded of and are learning to accept and willingly enter into your body's frailty, incapacity, and pain. You know the special graces as well as the terrible temptations to despair that illness brings, but you are going beyond these. You are coming to know that you are far more than your body.

The body is of particular concern to the older adult—it is of much more spiritual concern in later life than at any other time, except in situations where younger persons experience chronic illness, disability, or diseases in which there is protracted pain or incapacity. The temptations against hope that a painful body can cause in later life are far greater and potentially more serious than the physical temptations that the sexually driven younger person experiences.

It is very difficult for a person who has not experienced physical losses and pain to understand the tremendous effort that is involved in giving up the temptation to yield to a total, all-consuming interest in what is going on in one's body. I remember how I became caught up in inordinate concern for the physical well-being of the aged when I was younger and just starting out in my work with older people. I was on a community board with a number of older adults in various stages of physical difficulty. One 86-year-old woman, a former elementary school principal, had been a very active member of the board of this service and advocacy organization for a number of years. At one of the meetings she announced that she would not be attending the next three monthly board meetings. She did not volunteer the reason. We were all concerned for her. Because of my own narrow professional focus on illness and disease, I assumed that she was going to have surgery of some kind, probably hip replacement, as I knew that she was in almost constant pain due to damage done by rheumatoid arthritis.

So I asked her, in a very sympathetic (and probably condescending) tone of voice if there was anything I could do for her. She grinned widely and said with glee, knowing that she had "gotten" me, "Not a thing unless you want to help me with my baggage. I'm going on a freighter trip around the world!"

Needless to say, I was put (very nicely) in my place and learned an important lesson. But I was not satisfied to leave it at that. I *knew* this woman was in almost constant pain, and I wanted to know how she could possibly think of going on such a strenuous trip in that physical state. In addition I was aware that she was involved in volunteer work in many areas of the city on a daily basis. I wanted to know how she managed that, too. So I asked her. "Helen," I said, "I know you are in constant pain due to your arthritis. I also know you have had cancer of the colon and have had a colostomy—you have shared that openly with us. How do you continue to do all the things you do when you are in such pain?"

She replied, very thoughtfully and seriously. "You are right, I am in pain. And every morning I have the same decision to make—will I force myself to experience even more pain in the process of getting up, or will I let myself lie in my bed for the day? Believe me, it is no easy decision to make, because I have the freedom *not* to get up. But I force myself to go through the pain, to experience it fully and to go beyond it. I say to myself that I have the choice of being in pain here in my bed or as a volunteer usher in the Kentucky Center for the Arts. Believe me, I'd rather be in pain at the Center than in my bedroom. And do you know what? After I've been there for a half hour or so, the pain is much, much less. Sometimes I forget about it completely!" This process that Helen described is what research gerontologists call "body transcendence." It is a major developmental task of later life. And it is not an easy task to accomplish.

A New Radical Freedom

You may be realizing, however dimly, that in your innate poverty you are dependent on the gifts given. But this poverty which brings the need for gifts leaves you tremendously free. You have the security of memories of a lifetime of gifts bestowed—your own "personal salvation history." In later life you know you can depend on continued gifts, gifts appropriate to your age and situation. You know that you can trust that more gifts will be given. Thus, you are liberated to make a commitment to respond to the spiritual call of later life.

There is also a radical freedom from the constraints and expectations of society, a "rolelessness" in later life that does not exist at earlier stages of the life span. While dreaded by most people and perceived by social scientists as a negative occurrence, I believe that this "radical freedom of age" has a spiritual purpose. Its acute discomfort can become the impetus that liberates adults to go beyond the ordinary, the usual, the expected, to birth love in new and creative and courageous ways and to publicly model the message of love. Acceptance of this liberation is prophetic because it gives all older adults (and middle-aged people who fear their own aging process) a new and very different vision of aging.

Older adults who accept this freedom may be the ones who renew the face of the earth. In a lovely image used by my friend, Father Roy Stiles, they become "Advent people," symbols of those who wait in expectation for the coming of the Lord. And they birth the Lord in many different and rather unique ways, some as activists, some as contemplatives, praying for all the world from their nursing home beds. All the while waiting, pregnant with hope, icons of faith in the coming of Christ. Johann Metz, in *The Courage to Pray,* quotes Teilhard de Chardin. He says:

> "Again and again we continue to claim that we are waiting and watching for the Lord. But if we were honest with ourselves, we would have to admit that we no longer expect anything."
> Prayer can and must be the source which renews this expectation. It must stir us up against the annihilating hopelessness which undermines any commitment based on an ulterior motive. Hence Christianity's oldest prayer is simultaneously the most up-to-date: 'Come, Lord Jesus!' (Rev.22:20).

An activist/contemplative type person who exemplifies for me this wholehearted embrace of freedom to wait for just the right time to birth the God within is a woman who, in her mid-eighties, became concerned about the environmental consequences of deforestation after the death of her husband. At time of his death she went through a difficult time of grieving. She felt that her life held no meaning. She began to pray that she would be shown what God wanted from her for the rest of her life, however long that was to be. For no apparent reason she became interested in trees. She learned to categorize them. Then she began to read whatever she could about deforestation. She joined organizations dedicated to saving forests, donated money, and learned how to become politically active. Yet this was not enough for her. When she heard that a thousand-year-old redwood tree was to be felled for commercial purposes, she traveled to California at her own expense and chained herself to the tree in an actual and symbolic act of defiance.

Because she had trespassed on property owned by the lumber company, she was arrested and put in jail. She refused bond. When a reporter asked her why she, an elderly woman, was putting herself through this discomfort and embarrassment, she replied that for the first time in her life she was free to spend herself in any way she wished. In the past she could not afford to risk her life or her health on a single cause, no matter how important, because she was a mother, a wife, an employee. She was obliged to fulfill important roles that made her responsible to meet the needs of many others who depended on her. Now her husband was dead and her children were independent. She was no longer acutely needed by her immediate family but by the larger community—the earth itself. She embraced the gift of freedom and was willing to sacrifice her life because of the love she had developed for the planet. She gave birth to this love by the symbolic action of chaining herself to the tree and allowing herself to be imprisoned. She claimed that her courage emerged from her many years of spending time just "being with" God.

You do not need to chain yourself to a tree. You do not need to go to jail. (Unless you want to, of course.)

Ask for a Consuming Desire for God

But if you do feel even a twinge of genuine desire to enter into relationship with God with the depth, intensity, and totality I have described, the next step is to ask for the awareness of God's presence. Even if you are ambivalent about your desire, ask for more desire. How do you do this? In every way that you can possibly think of. As often as you can think of asking. With as much desire as your soul can muster.

There's an old story commonly told of one of the Desert Fathers. It seems that a young monk consulted an old and wise monk to learn from him how he could reach the awareness of presence and oneness with God. The old monk did not reply but asked the young fellow to come with him to the river. Once at the river he pulled the young monk into the water and held his head under for a long time. Just at the point of no return he let the young monk up for air. Dripping wet and gasping for breath, he was furious. "Why did you do that?" he shouted. "I was about to lose my life!" "When you desire God as much as you desire your own life and your next breath, then we can talk about how to be united with God," replied the wise old monk.

You may not yet feel such an all-consuming desire for God. In fact, at first you may find that your desire for such an awareness of God is ambivalent—full of fear and trepidation and maybe even dread. You are somewhat hesitant about the whole thing. Sometimes you want a closer relationship with God; sometimes you don't. This is both normal and realistic. The task at this point (if your yes outweighs your no) is to ask God for the desire for the gift of awareness of God's presence within. The desire will come.

It seems to me that the one prayer God could not possibly resist responding to is the request to come closer to God. Jesus instructed us to ask for whatever we need and has promised that we would receive. So we must enter our period of asking with an attitude of trust and belief. We believe that God wants to communicate with us, wants to be recognized, known, and loved. We believe that God wants us to be fully conscious members of the family of the Trinity, participating in that dynamic love. We believe that in order to be Christ-gift to others, we need this awareness. We believe this will be accomplished in us, that we will receive this gift of awareness, in God's own time and place.

After I read Thomas Merton and was awakened to the fact that awareness of oneness with God's Self was a gift that God offers to all who want it and decided that this is what I wanted for my life and to give back to life, I began what amounted to an harassment-of-God campaign. I became a real pest. I had one prayer, which I prayed as often as I could remember. At eighteen, I really didn't know exactly what I was praying for (still don't), but I knew instinctively that what I was praying for was what I desired more than anything else. I trusted that God knew what I wanted and would answer my prayer.

So pray. Ask. Beg. Not for very long, but very, very often. Stretch out your mind and heart and soul to God in yearning, asking for an awareness of God's presence. Let yourself feel the awful ache of God's apparent (but not real) absence. Then let go of your striving—and wait to see what happens. Be vigilant; remember those wise and foolish virgins (Matt. 25:1-13)!

Wait for God's Presence

The next step in preparation for receiving the awareness of the presence of God is to WAIT for it. The prior act of praying for the awareness of God's presence accomplishes two things. It helps you to focus your attention on God, and it heightens your sensitivity to the things of the Spirit, opening up your consciousness to signs of God's presence. You are on the alert, waiting expectantly, vigilant. You become like the pregnant woman who eagerly awaits signs of her baby's life, knowing that even in the tiniest flutter is the promise of maturity. So the next step on this journey is to assume an attitude of alert but relaxed attention. Mindfulness. You must cease your frenzied rush from one thing to another. Do one thing at a time, quietly, letting your mind and heart be filled with the gift of the present moment. Be completely present to whatever you are doing in the present moment. And begin to be present to—look around for—signs and symptoms of God within and without. We pride ourselves on being able to do two or more things at once—e.g. watch television and knit at the same time. But this fragments us. When we do more than one thing at a time we lose the ability to be present to one thing.

The signs of God's presence are there. The awareness of presence will come. But you yourself cannot force it, nor can you create it. It can't be imitated, faked. God acts in God's own time. The gift of God's Self is always present and constant within you if you are trying to love others and to be present to them as Jesus was to his friends. By your own efforts you can be present to others and experience their presence to you. But your conscious awareness of God's own presence, this Gift of Gifts, is above and beyond your power to provide for yourself. It truly is the entrance into eternal life; it is the kingdom of Heaven on earth, experienced in time. And it is pure gift, a gift you will receive once you realize you desire it more than any other thing on earth. However, you can prepare for it by imagining this presence, visualizing God there, by your side, talking with you, just "being with" you. These are excellent ways to prepare.

Do you really want God's total presence in your life? If you really do, in your waiting, prepare yourself for God's coming to you. Become an Advent person, awaiting the birth of Christ in your life. Be aware that:

- Now is the time to relinquish all you are attached to and give to the poor.
- Now is the time to admit that you cannot control God, your own life (or anyone else's), or your relationship with God.
- Now is the time to allow yourself to be led by Christ.
- Now is the time to acknowledge that you are poor in spirit, that you cannot create the kingdom for yourself. You have tried in the past but it didn't happen.
- Now is the time to be pure in heart. Kierkegaard said that "Purity of heart is to will one thing." You must will, then, only one thing—to open yourself to receive the awareness of the Trinity within.
- Now is the time, in Wesley's words, for "purity of intention and simplicity of affection."
- Now is the time to remember the story of the rich young ruler, recognizing that this is exactly where you are on your journey to God:

A member of one of the leading families put this question to him, "Good Master, what have I to do to inherit eternal life?" Jesus said to him, "Why do you call me good? No one is good but God alone. You know the commandments: *You must not commit adultery; You must not kill; You must not steal; You must not bring false witness; Honour your father and mother.*" He replied, "I have kept all these since my earliest days till now." And when Jesus heard this he said, "There is still one thing you lack. Sell all that you own and distribute the money to the poor, and you will have treasure in heaven; then come, follow me." But when he heard this he was filled with sadness, for he was very rich.

Luke 18:18-23

Now is the time to trust.

Will you follow the invitation to become another Christ-gift for the world?

What have you decided?

If your decision is yes;

if you acknowledge your innate poverty, granting that all is gift to be received and then given away;

if you desire above all things to follow Christ and are willing to be taught to love so that you can become a Christ-gift to the world,

then you will want and you will wait with empty hands outstretched.

Wait to receive, trusting that it will be given, for it has already been promised to you:

How happy are the poor in spirit;
  theirs is the kingdom of heaven.

Happy the pure in heart:
  they shall see God.
Matthew 5:3, 8

9

❧

INNER WORK:
REPENTANCE AND FORGIVENESS

For all its pervasive power, the growing magnetic force by which Christ draws us towards ever more intimate zones of his essence, is not sufficient by itself alone to attract us into his orbit.

If we are effectively to fall under the domination of Christ the centre of the world (king and centre of all things) we must of our own free will open our hearts to him. If we are really to enter into the chosen universe that is marked off around the incarnate Word, we must choose to form part of it.

Nothing, in the work of our "information" by Christ, can be finally effected so long as we are not freely co-operating in its realization.

Pierre Teilhard de Chardin, *The Prayer of the Universe*

IF YOU HAVE BEEN AWAKENED TO THE REALITY of the presence of God in your life and deepest being; if you have asked for and waited for an awareness of this presence and growth in oneness with God—even if your realization is not yet deeply felt and known, the work of nurture begins. I use the term *nurture* because all relationships must be nurtured or stewarded in order to deepen and develop. In most human encounters we start out as strangers and either remain in this state or advance to a relationship with some level of intimacy. So it is with our relationship with God.

There are a number of activities that are available to us to enhance our ability to be present to God and to receive the awareness of God's presence. I will present in these next few chapters the ones that I think are the most powerful and which can be used by people of all personality types. They include the inner work of *repentance and forgiveness, prayer, communion, spiritual reading, friendship, listening to God in other people, the remembering of life events, music,* and *nature.* It is up to you to try them out to see which "fit" you best. Keep in mind always that there are no rights or wrongs, betters or bests about this process. You are merely preparing the ground for the gift to be given and, when given, to grow and flourish.

Inner Work—The Next Step

Inner work—taking a long, hard, honest look into the depths of the mind and heart—is at the core of the offering of our lives to God. Without inner work there can be no truly intimate one-ing of our consciousness with the consciousness of God. We may come to an awareness of the Trinity within, but the ongoing development of relationship, of our growth in the family life of the Trinity, will not occur. It will not occur because there will be no opportunity for transformation. Only when we are willing to have our favorite and most entrenched, narrow ideas about God, ourselves, and others challenged are we open to being changed, transformed, and molded into the image of God. Only then are we able to become who we are in the eyes of God. As with all the gifts, this necessity, this urge, this desire to do inner work is a gift from God as we are drawn closer and closer to the center of ourselves, where the Trinity dwells. But we must choose to undertake this work.

What is inner work? It is just that—very hard work—a disciplined attentiveness, a "being with" ourselves and God, which takes place in our minds, hearts, and souls. It requires that we take a totally honest and close look at who we are and what we have been and want to be. It involves placing what we find into the hands of God. It involves being naked and standing in front of God, face to face, waiting for God to speak, to heal, to give direction, and, finally, to enfold us in loving arms and hug us.

Inner work involves three primary cyclical processes. I use the term *cyclical* because these processes are going on over and over again from the time of our awakening to the gift of the presence of God until death. They cannot really be separated from one another; the separation here is merely for the sake of description. The first part of this cycle is repentance; the second is forgiveness; the third is prayer—and not necessarily in that order, either.

Repentance

Let's look at *repentance* first. The word conjures into the imagination sackcloth and ashes, with maybe a little self-flagellation thrown in for interest. It's not a very popular word these days, for we don't like to think of ourselves as sinners. Products of dysfunctional families, yes, but persons hardly responsible for real sin. Nothing mortally dangerous. Nothing soul-killing. Yet, despite our inability to acknowledge sin we still don't behave very well towards ourselves or other people. Wars continue. We kill each other in body, mind, and soul in our families and our friendships, and in our relationships with strangers. We have very little trust, very little true intimacy, very little love in our lives.

Regardless of how "good" we are, we seem to be killing ourselves and other people in all kinds of ways, large and small, every day. If you don't understand what I am talking about, go into a grocery store and listen to the way some parents talk to their young children. Listen to the anger in their voices. Listen to the words as they cut the children down to size in an attempt to keep them in line. Go into many classrooms in the United States and listen to the words the teachers use when they talk to their students. Hear what the kids say back. It is no wonder that so many kids and teachers drop out of school.

Go into any house on your street and listen to the way husbands and wives bark at each other. Go into every nursing home in the land and listen to what the staff say to the residents, what they say to one another, and what the residents say to one another. What do *you* say to the driver who cuts you off on the expressway or the one who slithers into the parking space you were waiting for? I can't repeat here what I say. The point is, there is not much loving going on. Why don't we love one another? What on earth is wrong with us?

Let's go back to the Creation Myth for a hint of one possible answer. In my fantasy I imagine that Adam wasn't too pleased with Eve after they were flung out of their Garden plot. What a whopper of a fight that must have been. Perhaps Eve became the first abused spouse. Who knows? At any rate, I suspect that the family life of the First Couple of the Land was not all sweetness and light when they became homeless. Any respect they had had for one another went "down the tubes," as they say. Anger, bitterness, and mutual reproach, and an "I'm going to look out for number one from now on and get what's mine—you can fend for yourself," might have become the life themes.

As a society, I think we are in an "awakening" time in the history of sin through the ages. I do believe, as a person trained in the behavioral and social sciences, that we have learned both specific sins and patterns of sinning as a way to cope with our lives. We learned these behaviors from our parents and they from their own parents as far back as it goes. The basic sin is violence toward the other, which allows one to perceive the person as "other" rather than part of self. Spouse abuse and child abuse are good examples of this pattern of violence. Violent behavior is learned at home, and it proceeds from generation to generation. Often physical violence towards others is replaced by verbal or psychological violence. But it is still there, and it kills the mind and soul, if not the body.

In my psychotherapeutic work with older adults I am amazed at the number of both women and men who are victims of childhood sexual, physical, and/or psychological abuse. They seem to be coming out of the woodwork right now because for the first time in their lives they have words to describe what happened to them. I see them in the aged women who seem never to have grown up, who remain childishly dependent on anyone and everyone who will take responsibility for their lives. I see them in the elderly who are abusive of one another. I see them in the depressed older adults who will not respond to antidepressant and counseling therapy. I see them in those with memory loss who are letting themselves fade away into the oblivion of dementia. And I am not the only one recognizing these people. My male and female therapist friends are encountering the same phenomenon, and it is shocking to us. What happened? What is happening now?

Could it be that until this generation, until the awakening of social and personal civil rights in the last thirty years, the ownership of one's self with the rights and responsibilities that entails was not part of our evolutionary consciousness?

Could it be that, in terms of the evolution of thought and moral behavior, we have only just become persons, children of God, within the past thirty years? That before this time spouses and children were merely chattel, property to be used and abused and then thrown away as one saw fit? The American Humane Association was instituted many years before its counterpart, Child Protective Services, was developed. Before the child labor laws were enacted children were used for cheap and backbreaking labor. My own grandparents went to work in the Fall River cotton mills when they were nine years old. Many of their young cousins died of tuberculosis in their teenage years. Could it be that we humans valued our animals before our children? I think so.

What does this mean for us? It means that we are products of violence in our families, even peaceful families. How were you hurt? How did you hurt back? How do you continue to hurt others because that is what you learned early in life? Many of us hurt back by turning inward against ourselves. Nearly all of us were hurt in some way, for in the "olden days" violence in the family, in schools, and in society was not considered "abuse" or even "violence" because nearly everyone was engaged in it—it was the accepted mode of discipline. Now we are being called to look at it, to admit it, and to repent of it by learning new and loving behaviors.

How can we do this?

One story that gives me great hope for us all is that of a 93-year-old woman who was a member of a Presbyterian Church

Sunday School class I taught one day. My topic, as usual, was "Psychospiritual Growth in Later Life." When I came to the part dealing with the need for growth in our interpersonal relationships, she smiled animatedly and nodded her head. I knew this woman had a story to tell and gave her the floor.

"Well," she said, "I have been married and divorced five times. Only one of my husbands died, but that marriage wasn't a very good one, either. After the third relationship broke up I realized that it wasn't all their fault, that I must have had something to do with these divorces, too. My kids didn't turn out very well, either. One's in jail; the others live all over the country and don't have much to do with me. Can't say that I blame them.

"Well, when I was seventy I had a 'conversion' experience and joined the church. I guess I was afraid I was going to die soon. I changed some of my ways, but my relationships with other people didn't seem to improve much. I began to think that maybe I should get some counseling and learn how to treat people better. Maybe there was something really wrong with me. But I put it off because I was seventy, and I figured it was too late to change, that I'd be dying any day, anyway. I had confessed my sins to God, and I figured that was good enough. But I kept on living, and I kept on doing damage to people. I remarried at seventy-four, and that marriage ended up in divorce, too. Finally, when I hit ninety and found myself still alive, I realized, like you said, that I could end up living until I was 115. Decided I didn't want any more divorces and that I'd like to see my grandchildren, wherever they might be, and be a decent person for them.

"So guess what? At the ripe old age of ninety I got myself a therapist, and it's the best thing I ever did for myself. He helped me realize what I was doing to destroy others and myself over and over again. I realized that that was the way my parents had treated me and my brothers and sisters, too, and it was also the way I treated my kids. I am deeply, deeply repentant, for I wasted most of my life. But I am also deeply grateful to God for giving me one more chance to change and to be happy and to make other people happy. It's never too late to learn how to love!"

The message of the prophet Ezekiel is the message for our day in this place and in this time—knowing the failings of our ancestors we must now put them aside, for we are now responsible only for our own sins. We can be responsible not only by being aware of the ways in which our ancestors sinned against each other and against us, but by refusing to allow ourselves to fall into the same patterns of behavior. We now have the psychological technology to change our behavior; we *must* use this technology to enable us to learn new, loving interpersonal skills and to go and sin no more. No one living and mentally intact is exempt from this mandate. We are now ready to put into practice the teachings of Jesus. It has taken us hundreds of years to hear the message of love and to know how to respond to it as a society.

How are you sinning against your children? Do you inflict guilt, demanding that they promise never to put you into a nursing home? Do you refuse their help, claiming you never want to be put into the position of being a burden to anyone, yet creating more worry and burden by your fiercely independent stance?

How do you sin against yourself? Do you say you are too old to change, to grow, to remain a responsible member of society who needs to take a stand on moral issues? Do you take reasonable care of your body and mind, providing it adequate food, rest, exercise, medical care? Or do you say "I'm going to die anyway; who cares if I do such and such and die a little earlier?" The earlier dying might cost society thousands in insurance and you months of agonizing pain.

So we all sin, and we continue to sin into our old age. Yet we are all called to repentance, forgiveness, and the opportunity to learn new, loving behaviors.

How do we repent these days?

In all kinds of ways, some old, some new. The first step is to recognize our failure to love and our orientation to sin and to desire to change. This recognition we admit in the depths of our hearts to God. For most religious denominations this is enough. As a Catholic, a Methodist, a psychotherapist, and a sinner as well, I do think there is something else that is needed. I am convinced that we need to tell another human being of our failure to love. For

Catholics the Sacrament of Reconciliation was designed for this purpose. In the presence of God one tells an ordained minister of God—a priest—how one has failed to give and to receive love and how one may have destroyed love for another.

This is not an easy thing to do, for in this day and age we pride ourselves on independence and show only our best side to the public. That is why so few Catholics bother to use the sacrament any more. There is little understanding of the power inherent in being face to face with another human being in the presence of God, admitting to some failure to accept or give love. It is seen as being too embarrassing. It is humbling, intimate, and life-giving in a very unique way. The power isn't even so much in knowing or feeling that one is forgiven, but in publicly acknowledging that one has somehow "missed the mark" and needs to change; that one needs to learn how to love and needs help from God through another human being to accomplish this.

My own spiritual life had been full of ambivalence for a number of years, and I was stagnating at a confusing impasse until I came to terms with this need for repentance in my own life. I became aware of the need after I had been in psychotherapy for about a year, trying to deal with a post-traumatic stress depression I experienced after the accident with the truck. This depression brought into full light of awareness all kinds of learned sinful behavioral patterns, and I worked really hard on them in therapy with a spiritually oriented psychotherapist. But some unloving and downright destructive tendencies—my own greediness for achievement and public recognition, for example, which was making me insensitive to other people and causing me to take on too many unrelated and empty activities—would not budge. Even more serious, I became aware that there existed deep within me a certain perverse attraction to the dark things of life—more interest in others' pain than in their joy, with a corresponding inability to enter into their happiness. It was as if I could only "come alive" when dealing with suffering but could not relate to happiness. As a result, I would often reinforce in myself, friends, family, and patients a focus on suffering because that is when I would give them the most attention. This would keep them bound in suffering instead of liberated into joy. I understood the cause, the root of my sin, and I understood how I was perpetuating the sin, but I couldn't seem to stop behaving sinfully. Therapy had reached a standstill. What else was there to do?

I finally and wearily acknowledged as true for me a truth I had learned as information but had never understood with both my mind and heart—that the deeper I go into the wilderness of my self to find God, the darker and more serious are the sins I will find. The most powerful obstacles to the love of God for me will always be found closest to the center where God dwells. This is true because, in all likelihood, and under ordinary circumstances, I would never voluntarily search for God that deeply—deeply enough to bring such sin into the clear light of day. Given that admission, what was next?

I hadn't been to what used to be called "confession" for a number of years and had said publicly many times that I thought it a rather archaic sacrament and that psychotherapy was the modern version of the same process. A constant, insistent, inner tension prompted me to realize that this is what my soul required. I struggled for months against it. I kept saying to myself that the therapeutic discussion of these behaviors (sins) was enough, that formal "confession" of my sinfulness was unnecessary. But I was wrong; it was necessary. My sinful patterns of behavior had to be brought into the light of day before another human being, brought into the presence of Christ within that person, for healing to occur. And this person needed to be someone who knew me, not a "safe" stranger who would never set eyes on me again and to whom revealing my sin would not be very difficult at all.

Having repented and confessed these sins doesn't mean that I am rid of all this, because the tendencies toward these particular sins will continue to be part of my permanent psychological make-up—my "shadow side"—until I die. It does mean that I am more fully aware of when I'm about to get "hooked into" these behaviors, and I experience a greater freedom of choice related to what to do next. The attraction to pain, for example, can be transformed into the desire and action to healthily alleviate the pain of others. If it is not changed into such action, it becomes a powerful reinforcer of pain—my own and others'—another word for co-dependency. Awareness of my greedy need for achievement helps me to be able to say no to projects that do not relate to what I know I really must do with my life.

What do people who do not have a formal Sacrament of Reconciliation do? How can they have their need met for person-to-person confession of sins and reconciliation into the human community? Spiritual direction, counseling by clergy, or spiritual companioning and pastoral counseling are more and more widely used for this purpose. Most denominations recognize that we need one another and that God works for the good of each of us through our presence to one another. Confessing one's sins is more than looking for automatic forgiveness, but it is a plea for help to change behavior. We now have the psychospiritual technology; should we not avail ourselves of "experts"—spiritual counselors of one sort or another—to help us in our process of repentance and change? We seek help from all kinds of consultants for all manner of things from financial planning to hairstyle change. Why not consult a minister whose specialty is spiritual growth to help us in this process? Your own pastor is probably willing to help you in this. If he or she is uncomfortable in this role, have him/her suggest someone you can consult. God will lead you to someone, be assured of that.

Sometimes small Sunday School classes provide group spiritual companioning for one another. Our Beechmont United Methodist Church intergenerational class, the Good News Class, provides this for its members. It is informal, but we feel close enough to one another to reveal who we really are to one another. It has been a vehicle of repentance, forgiveness, healing, and change for most of us at one time or another.

If you are fortunate enough to have a "soul friend," a person to whom you feel able to bare the positive and negative sides of your most intimate self, he or she can help in this process of repentance. If she is a "soul friend," she is probably already doing so.

There are some areas that spiritual counselors are usually not trained to deal with. Those areas involve the more severe pathology caused by serious trauma in your childhood or early life or very difficult situations in your current life. For this you may need a trained psychotherapist—a psychiatrist, clinical psychologist, clinical social worker, or marriage and family therapist. If this is the case, make sure the person is licensed and certified and that you feel comfortable with him or her. It's perfectly fine and even advisable to shop around for the person you can relate to (but not necessarily the one who's going to be "easiest" on you). You do want to grow, and you don't want to waste your money, after all.

Forgiveness

Closely related to repentance is forgiveness—forgiveness of yourself and of other people. It is of special concern in later life, when all the hurts and failures of the past can suddenly flood you with so many unhealed, unresolved remembrances that you may feel overwhelmed by them. Guilt and bitterness result from the failure to forgive one's self and others. Let's talk about guilt first.

A successful physician on our faculty asked me to visit his eighty-three-year-old mother, Celia, in the nursing home, where she was recuperating from a mastectomy. The operation had been successful; the cancer had not spread to her lymph nodes, and her prognosis was very good. Yet she was very depressed, and he had no idea why. He stated, "She's led a very good life, has a husband who loves her, two sons who have been very successful, and she has not had a material need in her life. Her health is excellent, and she's in no real pain. She has absolutely nothing to be depressed about."

I went to the nursing home and introduced myself as a colleague of her son. I complimented his work and made the comment that she must be very proud of him. To this remark she lashed out at me in rage that she did not even try to temper, "That's what they all say—I must be so proud of him! Well, that's fine, but I'm the one who was supposed to be the doctor!"

Surprised, I asked her to tell me her story. It seems that she was a very bright youngster, and from the age of ten had wanted to become a physician. In the 1920s there were very, very few women doctors, but her family did not try to discourage her—they merely humored her talk of one day being a physician. She was graduated from high school and went on to college, majoring in chemistry. She had a straight-A average when, at the end of her third year, her father informed her that she could no longer attend college, that her younger brother would be the one attending college the following year. He said there was not enough money to pay for the tuition of both of them.

Celia said she had mixed feelings about her father's decision. The first was anger and despair, for she really wanted to go on to medical school. The second was a sense of relief. Most of her friends were married and had children by this time, and Celia felt at times that life was going on without her. In addition, she described herself as a "party girl" and she missed going to social events because she had to study. So she gave in to her father's wishes. Within a year she had married and in the next year gave birth to her first son.

During the course of the years her husband became a very successful businessman. They built a large home and entertained a great deal. She had another son. She was very attentive to husband, sons, entertaining, and charity work, but she always felt empty. She attended church, but this was for social and business purposes. After her husband retired both he and she started drinking heavily. She said that the alcohol numbed some of the pain some of the time, but that eventually it made her feel worse, so she stopped drinking. For years she had been existing, not really living.

Now, facing death, Celia was in despair. She could not forgive herself for not having become a physician. She said to me "Perhaps I am the one who was supposed to discover a cure for cancer! How many people in Eastern Kentucky (where the MDs are few and far between and where she wanted to practice) have died because I was not there to take care of them? I can't get this off my mind!" I and a crew of others, from psychiatrists to pastors, attempted to help her forgive herself, to help her see how she had contributed to life even though she had not been a physician. To no avail. Antidepressant medication was tried, without any success. Finally she died a very prolonged and bitter death, all because she refused to forgive herself for not accepting the "call" to become a physician. Celia's refusal to forgive herself affected her entire family and it left sad memories of a mother who felt that her life with them was of no consequence.

Do you have anything you need to forgive yourself for? I think we all do. We need to keep in mind that the necessary outcome of repentance is forgiveness. After we repent of what we have done to ourselves we need to ask forgiveness of God, others, and ourselves. Then we need to let go of our guilt, for the energy tied up in guilt can be better used for more life-enhancing activities. Often we are the ones who refuse forgiveness to ourselves, while God and other people have no trouble forgiving us at all.

In addition to forgiving ourselves in later life, we need to think seriously about forgiving all those whom we think have hurt us in some way during our lifetime. We need to come to the realization that we will never be totally healed from these hurts, but that they have shaped us into the persons we are. To the extent that we can forgive, this shape will be good and strong. Sort of like a bone that is broken and never set. Once the bone grows back, the arm may be misshapen, but it is as strong as ever—stronger in the area of the fracture itself.

I'm sure you know of people who have nursed a grudge for years and years. I had two aunts who feuded for years. They were the only surviving relatives on my father's side after he died. Always competitive with one another, they had argued about something silly and hadn't spoken for thirty years. Each kept up with the other's doings through cousins and other relatives and mutual friends, but each was firm in her resolution not to resume a relationship until the other apologized. I think, at the end, they forgot what they were fighting about. But neither gave in. Each died a lonely old woman, refusing to forgive the other. What could have been enjoyable years spent traveling and doing things they both liked to do were spent in spite and anger.

If you need to forgive yourself or other people and, try as you might, you just cannot let go of your anger, hurt, guilt, or other negative emotion, even though you have prayed about it, seek help from another person—preferably a therapist or a minister. Very often we cling to our hurts and anger because, in some strange way, they energize us and give our lives meaning. We say the person is not deserving of forgiveness. Maybe not, but that is not what is important. We are deserving of the freedom to let our hatred, our unforgivingness go. We are afraid that if we let our hatreds go there will be nothing to take their place—nothing to energize us, nothing to keep our minds well-occupied. It is easier to stay in a familiar state of hate than it is to learn to accept the gift of love and become a loving person. In the short run, hatred enlivens us, gives us energy. In the long run it will surely kill us, body, mind, and soul.

The time to forgive is now. People your own age are dying all around you; you may not have a chance to offer forgiveness to the person you need to forgive if you wait too long.

10

❧

INNER WORK:
PRAYER AND COMMUNION

ANOTHER PHASE OR PROCESS OF INNER WORK IS PRAYER. I almost hate to use the word because people have so often told me how they do not like to pray, how difficult it is for them, how futile it seems. Praying, which really could be the thing we most like to do in the entire world, usually becomes the thing we least like to do. So, often I use the terms *meditation, contemplation, being with, visualization, reflection,* anything that will ease the anxiety a little. But this is begging the point. Prayer is prayer. So what is prayer?

In my mind (and lots of people have many different definitions) prayer is simply being with God. It is taking the time to pull away from other concerns to deliberately attend to God, to listen to God's word to us, to allow God to love us and to teach us to love in return—by acknowledging God's existence in creation, God's activity in human lives, in beauty, and in suffering—any of these things and more. Practically, this means that when you suddenly notice a gorgeous tree while driving to the store, in your joy you acknowledge its Source with a "Thanks, Lord" spoken or unspoken. It means that at times you pull away from external work or play, even if they are the work of God, to pay attention, to be with God alone. For a few seconds, fifteen minutes, an hour, a day, a weekend, however long you both need to be together. But often, very, very often.

Have you ever watched a very young child, perhaps as early as eighteen months, explore her surroundings? Mother will be sitting there, perhaps talking with a friend in an environment that is not the home. The child will be immensely curious as to what is all around. At first she will cling to mother, insisting on sitting on her lap. Then, as she becomes more comfortable she will get off the lap and start to take a few steps into the room, perhaps going toward some interesting object. Suddenly she realizes that she has lost physical contact with mother. She panics and runs back. Mother reassures her that she is still there, and encourages her to continue exploring. She does, to her great glee. After a few minutes, suddenly she realizes again that she has forgotten about mother. She panics again, feeling alone and out of contact. She runs back for more reassurance that mother is there and still loves her. In the way this child is with her mother, so can we be with God as we venture into the vastness of the universe. God is present to us; God wants us to explore creation and delight in it. God enjoys our return, our "touching base"; God will give us another reassuring loving so that we can go back to face the world again, each time gaining in strength, courage, and our appreciation of creation and one another.

As I write this paragraph, I am in my fourth day alone at the cabin my husband Ron and I have been building for seven years at Nolin Lake, Kentucky. I have needed this solitary, concentrated time of "being with" only God for a long time. Shorter stretches of time have not been enough. I came in great fear, for I've never been here without my husband, and our cabin is relatively isolated. I've never been in solitude without some humanity nearby for this long a time. I didn't know if God would be able to keep me from climbing the walls of my own self. What I am finding is that God is here and that when I panic for any reason, I can keep running back to God's lap again and again and again.

I think the problem with prayer is that most people think it has to follow a prescribed form. We have to say certain words, sit still in a particular way, think specific thoughts, read only one kind of literature, and stay with it for a specified amount of time—in other words, adopt a certain "prayer behavior." The more I analyze the difficulties I have had over the years praying, the more I realize that we've put ourselves in prayer corsets, and it's time to take them off!

Most of us can't sit still for more than a few minutes at a time—and when we try to we get "antsy." Yet, we're told we must sit still for at least twenty minutes of prayer to "get anything out of it." What's to get? This is a way of "being," not doing or accomplishing anything. As we age the situation worsens, because sitting can be downright painful. The joints lock in place, the muscles stiffen up, the bones press hard against the chair. More often than not, we have to go to the bathroom. If not that, we go to sleep. What to do, Lord? For one answer I took a look at what I do when a dear, dear friend, Ellen Netting, comes to visit for a while from her home in the Arizona desert.

Like Being with a Friend

The first thing I do is *invite* my friend to come for a visit. Do you have any *true* friends who will barge in on your life for a significant amount of time uninvited? No, they respect your privacy. God likes to be invited. The next thing I do is spend some time "nesting." I make sure the surroundings are comfortable and non-intrusive. I put on the telephone answering machine. I make sure we're both physically comfortable. If we're wearing formal, workday, uncomfortable clothes, and she's brought her grubbies, we both get into casual clothes. If we're hungry, I scurry around getting us something to take the edge off hunger, but not enough to distract us with a feeling of fullness. I look for the room which is most conducive to good conversation, where I know we will not be disturbed by other people, traffic noises, and housework begging to be done. If I am in the least agitated, I choose the rocking chair, to soothe me and center me quickly with its repetitive motion. If I'm in the mood, I'll let a cat sit on my lap, allowing the purring to calm me down. I let Ron know that we're visiting and need some private time and that he can join us later. Now, and only now, am I ready to listen to my friend, to pay attention, to "be with" her with all of my mind and heart and strength. I have prepared myself for her visit.

Now, if she's staying for the weekend, she must realize that I can't sit with her all day and all night. So while I cook and clean or do whatever it is I have to do I sit her in the room wherever I am, listening to her and talking to her, being present to her, while I do my chores. This is fine with Ellen.

Sometimes, after all the talking and sharing, and catching up on what we've both been doing, she just wants to rest; we're "talked out." So we might just enjoy the fact that we are in one another's presence, in this place and in this time. We might listen to music together, read books, pet the cats, make "friendly plastic" earrings, swing on the swing, take a walk, sit on the grass watching the boats on the lake—or just sit. Nothing more is said. We are just there with one another, enjoying the fact that we are friends, sharing one another's lives, grateful that we live on this planet at the same time, loving one another. That is more than enough.

So it is when we visit with God for any length of time. We start out with some mental and physical agitation. But if we nest a little, do and say what feels comfortable, sooner or later we'll come to the point of just resting in one another's company. And that is the very best part.

Sometimes, when I'm expecting a visit, my friend fails to come, for one reason or another. This is a disappointment. What is wrong? Why is she not here yet? All kinds of disturbing thoughts cross the mind. Remembering that she said she would come if she could, I calm down, go about my tasks, and keep her in the cradle of my mind. I can't imagine where she is or what she is doing, but somehow she is present to me; I know she would be here if she could, and that is enough. She is in my heart.

When You Can't Feel God's Presence

So it is with God. Often we don't "feel" or recognize God's presence, sometimes for a very long time. This can be disturbing, and some folks think they are not praying "successfully" or that

God is angry with them and has abandoned them for some reason. Not so. Because God exists, God is present. For whatever reason, God couldn't come in person today to our personal consciousness —perhaps because of distractedness, mood changes, pain, preoccupations—any number of things. So we keep God in our hearts, knowing that God will come to us at some time and in some way—the door is open.

Prayer is nothing more and nothing less than resting in the presence of God, "being with" God. Whatever else happens flows from that "being with"—whether it be adoration, petition, intercession, praise, or thanksgiving. How you enter into God's presence is your own business. Don't let anyone tell you that your way is not the right way. Also, don't try to force yourself to be with God in any particular way. For example, do not force or try to create loving feelings. Your lack of feelings does not mean that you do not love God and vice versa. Merton has written that prayer is best learned in the times of dryness and boredom, when your heart feels stone cold. If you can stay with God in these times, you'll have no problem in the times of joy, when God feels near.

If you can't form a mental picture of Christ present, that's fine, just stay with him in a kind of darkness. If that's frightening or distressing to you, you could think of yourself as being in a dark room, where you can't see or feel the presence of Christ or anyone else, but you know that he is there even though your senses of sight and hearing don't perceive him. In fact, as we age, and as we spend more and more time in prayer whatever our age, we tend to lose our ability to visualize, imagine, or form mental images. This can be very distressing to people who have long enjoyed imagining themselves in scriptural scenes or have pictured Christ right alongside of them. Many feel that God has abandoned them or that something is wrong. Not so. It is a natural phenomenon, one that is important to "wait out."

If you stay with God in faith, in the stark belief that God is, indeed, present to you even though you can't "feel" or perceive the presence in any way, you are doing what any devoted friend would do. You are sticking by your friend, and that's all you can do. It is like being with Christ in Gethsemane again and again, where he wants and has asked for your presence but is so involved with his own crisis (which is for *your* welfare) that he can't consciously concentrate on his immediate relationship with you at all—but he wants and needs you to be there with him.

Attempting to "be with" Christ in Gethsemane and the knowledge of his "absent presence" has been the main source of my own ability to stay with prayer throughout my life, for only rarely have I felt that I "experienced" the comforting or joyful presence of God in prayer. In encounters with other people, in liturgy, in nature, in events, in music, in ordinary life—yes—but rarely in prayer. In prayer I experience primarily absence. But I believe it is the time spent in prayer, being with God, that enables me to become aware of Christ at all the other times—in people, events, situations, nature, reading, etc. What happens to me in prayer is that that is when God helps me realize the barriers I have put up to prevent myself from being loved by God, others, and myself. Sometimes we will be aware of presence; sometimes we will not. It doesn't matter. What matters is the being with, making one's self available to God.

Overwhelmed by God's Presence

What about the times when you feel overwhelmed by feelings, when you actually seem to be overtaken by feelings that you perceive, intuitively, to be related to the presence of God? This was Wesley's experience at Aldersgate, when, as he put it, "I felt my heart strangely warmed." Obviously, he was surprised by the experience, as you may be if and when this or something like it happens to you. One of the questions many people have is, "Is this really the presence of God?" The question is asked because the feeling is so intense, and so related to the process of "being with" God in or out of prayer, that they do seem connected. This can also happen when you are in the midst of nature, enjoying a sunset, for example. You suddenly feel overwhelmed with joy and pleasure by the beauty of the scene. You feel connected to it in a way you hadn't felt connected before. Some women report having this experience during childbirth. Some say that they have experiences like this while making love or listening to a beautiful piece of music. However or whenever it occurs, it is intense and brings the person into Presence where one feels part of everything that is. You might feel greatly loved. Wesley became convinced of God's "saving" love for him through this kind of an experience.

The mystics have described such experiences for hundreds of years. Recently scientific researchers have studied the phenomenon. They found that many, many people have had at least one experience of feeling overwhelmingly loved or having been caught up in tremendous beauty. Children seem to have a great capacity for such experiences. The problem is that we adults are often embarrassed by such experiences because they are not "rational," cannot be easily explained, and, while they are happening, we are pretty much out of control. And we do so love to be in control! So we don't nurture these experiences by sharing them with one another; we keep them to ourselves or throw them away as something inconsequential.

One of the problems is that there are few words in our vocabulary that we can use to describe what we have experienced. So "we trip in fumbled wordings" and eventually give up any attempts to share these experiences, even with intimate friends.

Another thing that can happen in an experience like this that may frighten some people is that intense sexual feelings can be aroused. How can we reconcile an intense feeling of "being with" God with sexual feelings? When this happens, some people begin to think there is something wrong with them, or that they are sinning in some way. It is so distressing that they give up praying entirely. What is happening to us when this occurs?

Basically, the body is not a very good differentiator of what is going on in our minds. Let me give you a few examples. Have you ever been so enthusiastic and excited about an idea or an event that you felt you had to go to the bathroom? Suddenly your bladder or intestines reacted to whatever your mind was experiencing. Have you ever felt so nervous that you experienced the same thing? Do you blush when you are embarrassed? Do you lose your appetite when you are sad? Have you ever broken out in a cold sweat of fear? Have you ever been sexually aroused by the presence of another person? I would venture to say we have all experienced a few of these physiological responses to primarily mental events—we are all human beings and this is how the body is designed.

When we are in a loving relationship with God and our minds become full of the realization of God's love or beauty or grandeur or power—or whatever—our body will often react in some way. This reaction can run the gamut from a feeling of gentle peacefulness and warmth to intense joy, sexual arousal, all the way to an ecstasy, where one seems to not even be in one's body for a while. These experiences in and of themselves are not God. They are the body and mind's physiological reaction to the awareness of God's presence. They occur because we live in our bodies and our bodies don't have a special "organ" for relationship with God (except maybe that part of the brain we talked about earlier). If these experiences do not occur, it does not mean that God is any less present to us. In fact, as we grow in our prayer lives they will occur less and less, until we rest, ultimately, in the dark, imageless, sensationless Presence. It is almost as if we are programmed to respond on the pleasurable physiological level first, so that our minds will be converted, and we will want to dedicate all of our lives to loving service as Christ-gift.

So whatever you feel or don't feel during prayer, take it all with a grain of salt. Avoid getting addicted to the good feelings, and don't criticize yourself when you can't sense God with you. You are no closer to God when you are sensing God's presence than when your heart is stone cold. God is present to you whether you physiologically, emotionally, or intellectually perceive and react to this or not. Receive whatever experience the awareness of God evokes in you as gift, to be accepted, acknowledged with gratitude, nurtured, then relinquished, shared with others through your loving service to the body of Christ.

So the message about prayer is this:

(1) *Prepare your surroundings.*
(2) *Relax your body.*

(3) *Do whatever you need to do to be comfortable*—rock, dance, walk (yourself or a dog), knit, garden, cook, clean house, pet a cat, listen to music, deep breathe, repeat a favorite word, sip Japanese tea, sew, arrange flowers, hold a sleeping grandchild, do Tai Chi, canoe, fish, swim, or just sit— WHATEVER you want to do.

(4) *Be with your God*. Be with Christ in a Gospel story. Be with him in your mental space, as he visits you. Invite him to spend time. Let him know the door is always open for his visit, the teapot is always on. Your house is his house, to relax in, to take a nap in. To just be himself in. Let your place be a place where he knows there are no demands. Just gentle, peaceful loving companionship that can be silent.

(5) *Just do it*. Often. Very often. Let yourself look forward to the visits. Anticipate. Prepare. Look for him. Be always ready for his appearance. He will come. He needs hearts that want his company, that are ready to be with, to listen, and to suffer with Him. You can give Christ friendship. The only thing that Christ asked for himself from his disciples was that they stay awake and keep him company in the Garden of Gethsemane. Think of yourself as doing that, being there for him in the silence of his agony.

(6) *Don't worry about how or what you are feeling,* if anything. Accept whatever experiences are given as gift.

(7) *Do not compare your prayer with that of another*. Share, yes, but don't evaluate yours by the standards of another. If you do, you will probably end up believing that the other person is a better "pray-er" than you are and become discouraged.

Try this meditation.

Get comfortable and relax. Take a few deep breaths.

Now imagine yourself sitting at your kitchen table at your favorite time of day, when you are all alone in the house. Picture what the room looks like. Imagine what it smells like. What is the lighting like? Get a good image in your mind of that kitchen. Feel how the chair feels under you, how the floor feels under your feet. Be there for a minute or so.

Now imagine yourself hearing a knock at the back door. What does it sound like? Visualize yourself wondering who it is, then getting up to answer the door. At the door, waiting for you to open, is Jesus. He says you have been on his mind and that he has come to visit for a little while. Is that all right with you? Imagine how you feel when he asks you that question. What do you say to him?

You invite him into the kitchen and offer him a chair at the table. You offer him coffee, some toast. You are nervous and bustling around, not quite knowing what to say or do. Gently, he calls your name. "Just pour us a cup of coffee," he says, "and come and sit down and let's visit." You sit, nervous at first. He takes a sip of coffee and smiles contentedly. "That's wonderful," he says. Slowly you relax. He sits comfortably and is at ease, just enjoying being in your presence. He is totally available to you, totally open to whatever you have to say to him.

What do you want to say? Go ahead and share whatever it is you want to share of yourself. This is your very best friend, the one who is the Center of your life, who has chosen you and who wants to spend this time with you. What does Christ say to you?

Know that being with Christ is of value not only to you and to Christ because when you are with God in this way, you bring with you all of the members of the body of Christ. You bring them with you into the presence of Christ to be healed and loved, strengthened and nurtured, even if you are not aware of doing this. This is "work" of the most intense kind, work that transforms not only you but the entire world; for in your prayerful companionship with God you bring comfort to the world in ways you will never know.

As an older person you are specially called to this kind of work. It does not matter where you are or what shape you are in. This life of prayer is available to all who desire it. Even if you are lying paralyzed in a B-grade nursing home you can, through this kind of prayerful companionship with God, send the prayerful energy of love out into the farthest reaches of the universe.

All time is prayer time, not just the few formal minutes we sit in conscious company with God. Eventually, if we are faithful to the formal time, we will come to realize that we are praying constantly, that the awareness of God in our minds and hearts has become continual without our even being aware of it and that it feeds our other activity—it becomes the source of our thoughts and actions.

Communion

Jesus himself gave you the very best gift to prepare yourself for continual awareness of God within and for transformation into his own consciousness. This gift is that of the Eucharist, Holy Communion, the eating of the body and the drinking of the blood of Christ.

From a purely psychological and physiological standpoint, this gift is incredibly powerful. We know that what we eat and drink daily becomes a part of us. We know that different kinds of foods have different effects on us. We also know that the acts of eating and drinking are pleasurable. The intensity of this pleasure enables us to put in the effort to prepare food and eat again. We know that if we do not eat or drink we will die. Therefore, we must eat and drink to maintain life, to grow to the fullness of our physical potential, and to experience a significant degree of physical and emotional comfort. We also know that the first meal we ever enjoyed was eaten in the company of another—our mother fed us from the food of her own body. This process of feeding and being fed established an intimate, nurturing bond of love that our subconscious memories will associate with food itself and with the act of eating and drinking until the end of our lives.

So it was not by accident that Jesus chose to connect the basic, almost universal foods of bread and wine with his own body and blood. There is no other act which would symbolize as well the presence of the Trinity within, transforming us into Christ.

Sexual imagery is found in scripture and in the writings of some of the mystics to symbolize the union of God with the soul. But even sexual union is not as complete as is the simple (yet incredibly complex) act of eating, digesting, and transforming food into one's selfhood, for the elements of food nourish every single cell of our body. In addition, unlike sexual union, which we do not need to engage in, we do need to eat and drink, and to do this often, at least once every day in order to adequately maintain our lives.

Jesus was physically concrete, knowing that we need to use our senses to come to him. We are material beings and relate first to the material world. Because of this we need the physical to enable us to remember that we are loved. Who can keep in mind an abstract idea like love? Few of us, for any length of time. But even young children and the mentally disabled know that when they are fed, someone is loving and nurturing them. So Jesus used food as a love symbol of himself because he knew that we had already made the memory connection between food and love, when we were first fed by our own mothers.

The food Jesus chose to symbolize his embodied love was something basic to the life of most cultures and something that we can see, taste, touch, smell, and even hear. We can see the color, texture, and roundness of a loaf of bread, touch its firm pliancy, feel its texture, hear it being ripped apart, smell its yeastiness, taste its sweetness. We can see the rich amber color of wine, touch its wetness, hear its fluidness when it is poured out, smell its grapeness, taste its tartness. Bread and wine are simple and real. Even without their association with the body and blood of Christ they are nourishing.

But when they are intentionally made into reminders of Christ's love, his body dedicated to life and broken in the process of his trying to teach us how to love life in ourselves and others, and to become aware of his oneness with all of us, what power they have to transform us! How can bread and wine do this? First, Jesus told us that the bread and wine represented himself, his fullness of being, and that they represented the love of God for us. We are being asked to make a deliberate and conscious leap of the imagination into a different mode of reality when we accept this assertion. Second, he told us to remember him—who he is and the Father's love he made available to us, and how he taught us to love one another—whenever we eat this bread and wine. So not only do we have the benefit of the actual substance of the bread and wine nourishing us, we also have the memory of Jesus' life, work, and loving that transforms our consciousness. How does this transformation happen? Primarily through the leap of the imagination into a different reality that was mentioned above. This leap, too, has its counterpart in human presence.

Do you remember ever having been so head-over-heels in love with someone that you thought about that person all the time? You carried your loved one in your heart so constantly that he or she actually seemed present to you. You held imaginary conversations with him or her. You will remember that you imitated the person, watching what he or she did and said, how she moved, what he thought, etc. You watched all the tiny little details and both consciously and unconsciously imitated her behavior in order to be like that person. You loved that person so much that you wanted to be just like him. Your remembrance of her kept you imitating her even when she was not present to you. The love did not even have to be known, acknowledged, or reciprocated by your beloved for you to be changed by your love for that person. But when that love was indeed returned, how much more powerful and wonderful it was because you were both being transformed by your mutual care and involvement in one another's lives.

The very same thing can happen to us when we intentionally remember Christ and the totality of being he offers us. He created a new reality for us so that we will be encouraged to enter into this ritual of remembering often. Let's look at the words of the Communion service from the United Methodist Hymnal:

When the Lord Jesus ascended,
he promised to be with us always,
in the power of your Word and Holy Spirit.

On the night in which he gave himself up for us,
he took bread, gave thanks to you, broke the bread,

gave it to his disciples, and said:
"Take, eat; this is my body which is given for you.
Do this in remembrance of me."

When the supper was over, he took the cup,
gave thanks to you, gave it to his disciples, and said:
"Drink from this all of you;
this is my blood of the new covenant,
poured out for you and for many
for the forgiveness of sins.
Do this, as often as you drink it,
in remembrance of me." [italics mine]

Jesus wants to be remembered over and over until the remembrance is an integral part of our identity—what we know to be our "selves"—transforming our "selves" into his own. And not only does this loving remembrance change our individual identity, it also changes the identity of the body of Christ, for when we become more Christ-like, the body becomes more complete. Christ is just a tiny bit closer to coming in glory, the kingdom one step further in coming to fruition here on earth. Christ wants us to remember that he came into being for each one of us, to teach us how to receive love from the Father, and to teach us how to be present in love to ourselves and to each other. Because we are so enmeshed in the blindness of greed and the vision of personal isolation the world promotes, we must have something tangible to bring back to mind the fact that there is a spiritual, loving reality that supersedes the reality of the physical world. So he combined the material with the spiritual in choosing bread and wine to represent himself. In addition, these simple elements are available to the poorest of us—they are not silver and gold, available only to the wealthy.

In the same way that we bonded with our mother when she breastfed us, we bond with Christ when we eat the bread and wine. When we share the bread and wine we also bond with one another, for Christ's presence in us pulls us all together in love. So this communion is simultaneously a connection with the Father, Son, and Spirit, a connection with our own true selves, and a connection with one another as brothers and sisters in Christ.

How often is communion offered in your church? In some it is once every four months. In others it is once a month. At the Older Adults Ministries conference held at Lake Junaluska in the summer of 1992 there was a communion service offered each morning. A significant number of the 350 people present attended, even though it was scheduled for 7 AM. The presence of Christ was palpable in the atmosphere of the chapel. It is obvious to me that there is a real hunger for the food that is Christ.

If your church does not offer communion often, what can you do to compensate? There are a number of things, both obvious and subtle. Here are a few—create others using your own imagination.

(1) Request more frequent communion services, on Sundays within or separate from the usual service or during the Wednesday evening potluck suppers and/or Bible studies.
(2) Each meal you share with your friends or family members could become a meal of remembrance. We often say grace before meals. Why not repeat the words of Christ, asking the Spirit of Christ to be represented in the food you are eating?
(3) You can have a special offering of bread and wine/juice as part of a prayer group or other meeting.
(4) Whenever you offer food to another, you can consecrate it to the memory of Christ.
(5) Any time you share food with anyone think of it as the breaking of bread with Christ present to you.

Privately (or they'd think I was totally off the wall, not just halfway off) I bake, dedicate, and offer chocolate chip cookies to my friends in this way. Chocolate chip cookies have had deep significance for me since childhood. When I was five years old I had rheumatic fever and was confined to bed for a year. There were no other children in the family, and I was out of contact with all the kids in the neighborhood, except for one, Pammy Glynn, a twelve-year-old girl who lived next door. Pammy came home from school every Friday afternoon and baked chocolate chip cookies for her family. Just before supper each week for a year she would bring to our house a little plate of them, just for me. My mother allowed her to stay for no more than five minutes, and her visit was the only contact I was allowed to have with someone of my own age each week. These were the best five minutes of the entire week! I spent a lot of time waiting for her, looking forward not only to the cookies, but, most of all, her presence. Pammy's visit, bearing the cookies, was, in every sense of the word, *Eucharist*. It was a Eucharist celebration. She came in love, and because of that love, Christ was present to us. As children, we weren't conscious of this presence, but our "being with" was important to us, and I think we both reaped the benefits of God's love. (And the cookies were so very good—I still remember the taste and have not been able to duplicate them.)

An older member of our congregation told me of an unexpected experience of communion he was gifted with one Saturday morning in our neighborhood. He was meandering through the booths of the neighborhood's Spring Flower Festival early on a Saturday morning. One of the women's circles had a booth at the festival and was selling homemade bread, and he bought a full loaf of bread to munch on. To his delight it was the same recipe that we use for our communion service—very delicious bread. As he wandered from booth to booth, eating bread and looking at all the stuff, he would notice a stranger or a friend here and there watching him eat. Every once in a while someone would say, "That looks like good bread!." To this he would reply, "Yes, it's wonderful. My church group made it. Break off a chunk so you can taste how good it is." At this point he would let them rip off a piece for themselves. Some then went to buy their own loaves. He said that never had he felt so one with other people as during that morning's walk. It was truly an experience of Eucharist for him.

When you begin to be aware of how Christ is present to you in the materials of bread and wine, your consciousness of his presence will expand. You will find yourself beginning to remember him in other things. You will begin to recognize him in all people, including yourself.

11

❦

INNER WORK:
READING, PEOPLE, AND LIFE EVENTS

Spiritual Reading

ANOTHER APPROACH TO ALLOWING GOD TO BE PRESENT to your awareness is to start to read scripture slowly and meditatively, knowing that the word of God rests in those pages for you. This means that instead of selecting a passage of scripture you want to read and study and "accomplish" something with, take a different approach. Select a passage and read it very slowly, letting yourself absorb the beauty and meaning that each word, each phrase holds for you.

Do any phrases resonate with your own experience? Do any evoke feelings, either positive or negative? Savor each phrase. If something strikes a chord in your heart or mind, if it seems to have particular beauty or meaning for you and your life situation, stay with it, be with it, let it permeate your whole being. Bring your presence to it. Let the word of God be present to you. If you are particularly inclined to skip over a passage, stop and spend more time with it. Where is your resistance to the passage coming from? What message are these words speaking to you? What is God telling you through your mental and physical reaction to the words?

How do you know that what you have read is relevant to your situation? A flash of insight, a sudden sense of affection, a feeling of relevance, a warmth, even an aversion—all of these are a quickening of the God-life within you.

Mattá al-Miskin, a Coptic monk who lives in the desert monastery of Deir el Makarios fifty miles southwest of Cairo, has written in his book, *The Communion of Love,* of the transforming and unifying effects of reading scripture in this way:

> When we read the books of the Bible, they appear outwardly to be purely a history of temporal events. But if we consider deeply their purpose and aim, and relate ourselves to what we read, we discover that they intend to reveal the living God Himself in our own selves. We see ourselves as we are, and then we begin to see God as He is, especially when He is compared with us. What is the value, then, of God's being revealed to man? In this lies the whole secret of the Torah and the Gospel, and the essence of the value of humankind and the whole of history. "And this is eternal life, that they know thee the only true God, and Jesus Christ whom thou has sent" (John. 17:3).

In addition to scripture, any reading can be used in this way. It does not need to be a religious book; it can be a novel or poetry. It is the intent with which you read that makes the difference. For example, you could read a novel for pure fun and pleasure and stress reduction or for the deeper meaning of the words. Sacred reading is just that—it looks for the sacred in the words on the page. The children's books of Madeleine L'Engle are sources of profound spiritual insight for me, and, as I stated before, the reading of Thomas Merton's book *Seeds of Contemplation* awakened me to the life of the Spirit. May Sarton, Annie Dillard, Wendell Berry, Robert Coles—these are some of the authors who are deeply spiritual and have touched my life. There is for me in their works a communion of spirit that transcends the printed pages and reaches out to embrace me in love.

I think that of all the spiritual "exercises" available to us, sacred reading has been the single most important one in the development of my own life with God. The reason for this rests primarily in the type of personality I have, not in the value of the exercise itself. And because it so quickly brings me into the presence of God, I must be careful not to depend on it too completely. So I push myself to expand to other ways of being with God, asking myself what I would do if I could no longer see or understand the printed word. You may not resonate with sacred reading very much at all, and that is perfectly OK. Feel free to experiment and explore—search and find what is best suited to your needs.

Other People

Being attentive to the people all around you is another way to be open to God. What you may find is that you are much more aware of the presence of God in other people than you are in yourself. That is fine, for the Trinity dwells in others as in you—this is the basis of the concept of the body of Christ. So watch how other people live and love. Watch them pray. Listen to what they say.

What are people saying to you—*really* saying to you underneath all the superficial talk? What is God within them trying to communicate to you? Their words probably will not be traditionally "religious" but may have some significance to you, affirming you, correcting you, encouraging you, instructing you. Ada, a slightly retarded elderly friend of mine who is homebound, has a special ministry she has adopted on her own. She sends birthday cards to people she has met and been touched by in some way through the course of her life. Some of these people belong to her church; many others are now in nursing homes. Every once in a while she wonders whether she should give up this ministry because of the growing expense of stationery and postage. But she told me recently that just when she starts harboring thoughts of giving it all up, inevitably someone will call and say to her "You just don't know how much it meant to me to receive your card and message. I had come to the point where I felt that no one cared, no one thought about me any more and that I might as well just give up when I received your card. I feel connected to life again. Thanks so much." What is God telling her through this lady? Ada believes God is saying something like, "I heard your complaint and I understand the cost. But do you see now how important this seemingly insignificant work is, how it keeps love in the world just a little bit? I would like you to keep doing it, no matter what the cost." The lady who thanked her for the card said one thing; God helped my friend interpret these words as encouragement for her ministry.

Sometimes God corrects us through other people. I recently had my hair cut after wearing it in a bun for twenty years. For a while I was regretting the decision to do this and thinking about how long it might be before I could grow it long enough for the bun again. I had liked the look because it was inexpensive, easy to care for, and looked quite a bit different from other hairstyles. However, about fifteen years ago a professor who was supervising my clinical work advised me to get rid of it. She had said then, "If you're going to be a psychotherapist, you'd better get rid of that hairstyle. It's too severe and it puts distance between you and other people. Get it cut or wear it down!" I was insulted and paid no attention to her. In fact, to be perfectly honest, I liked that idea of the distancing effect. Then, shortly after I did get it cut, at a party welcoming our new medical students, one of our young staff members—someone I hardly knew and had rarely even talked to— came up to me and said, "I hope you don't think I'm being too personal, but I want to tell you something about your hair. Before you cut it I was afraid to talk to you—you seemed so cold and distant. Now you're friendlier. I feel as though I could just come up to you at work and say 'Hi'."

Now, I could have taken his words as both a criticism and a compliment and left it at that. But coming at a time when I was experiencing a great deal of confusion, I paid attention to the words and pondered the comment for God's message. I decided to open up my awareness to what God was saying to me. And it was plenty. What I understood or interpreted the young man's words to mean was the following, "Janie, look very closely at your need to be and to look different. This narcissism is a barrier to our relationship and to my ability to love other people through you. Let yourself experience the poverty of ordinariness, for one of the temptations you need to deal with is the world's message that you are not good enough, you cannot be loved unless you are different, better, or special in some way. Each person is unique and special to me. Each person reflects a different aspect of my creative love." A profound message through a seemingly casual, everyday comment. Yet it opened up a whole new area that I needed to examine—an area that has long been a barrier to my ability to receive God's love and to my ability to be an instrument of God's love for others by being present and available to them—by being one with them.

What has God said to you through other people lately? Have you listened? Spend a day soon just paying close attention to what people really say to you. Open your mind and heart to the message that God might be trying to get across to you.

Someone once asked me how we know when God is "speaking" to us. Do we hear special words uttered in some strange and different way? I don't really have a good answer for this, except to say that what you hear, whether from another person, in what you read, or in what you are thinking in your own mind will somehow strike a chord of meaning for a particular situation you are dealing with at a specific time. The truth of the message will "hit home," usually on an emotional as well as an intellectual level. When you allow yourself to be open and put some effort into paying attention to God's voice within and without, when you actually want to hear what God has to teach you, and believe that the message will come, you will recognize the message, just as Ada did. You may feel it in the pit of your stomach or you may get a flash of insight, but it will be there for you. It may be a kind of "Aha" experience. Sometimes it will be repeated over and over again from different sources before you start paying attention to it. (I usually have to be confronted with it many times before I get the message.)

God most often speaks to our hearts in very ordinary, commonplace ways. In 1963, the year my mother was dying, there were three new popular songs that I felt to be God "speaking" to me, consoling me, assuring me that in time all would be well with my life. They were so popular that our music director, Paul

Gazagian, chose them as selections for our Mixed Chorus spring concert at Somerset High School. To my great joy, not only could I listen to them on radio and record, but I was able to sing them with a large group of students, among whom were many of my friends. We practiced three times a week from 7:00 till 8:30 in the morning from January until May.

For months these songs inspired me and gave me the courage to keep going, until they finally became the only prayer I could utter, silently, in the depths of my heart. Their titles were "No Man Is an Island," "Climb Ev'ry Mountain," and "You'll Never Walk Alone"—just exactly what I needed to hear over and over again that desolate fall, winter, and spring. After seven months of agonizing illness my mother died in despair in March, refusing to the last to write a will and to appoint a guardian for me. Through all of the legal chaos that ensued and the difficulty finding a permanent place to live, the songs kept me company and encouraged me to look forward to my future life. The following June I entitled my graduation speech "No Man Is an Island." Later I "found" another Thomas Merton book, *No Man Is an Island,* in a college bookstore. Coincidence? John Donne wouldn't think so! These songs are still prayer for me, and whenever I feel discouraged I continue to play my ancient and well-scratched recording by the Lettermen.

Robert Coles has more than a few words to say on this subject of God speaking to us. Coles (my new hero since Merton's death —I seem to have to have modern-day, real-life spiritual heroes and heroines to keep me pointed in the right direction) is a professor of psychiatry and medical humanities at Harvard University. He has written a wonderful book entitled *The Spiritual Life of Children,* in which he draws from thirty years of interviews with children all over the world to describe their inner spiritual and religious experiences. In an interview with Avram, a twelve-year-old conservative Jewish boy from an affluent suburb of Boston, the two discuss how Avram "hears" God's voice.

As I listened to Avram, I [Coles] wondered: Exactly whose voice does he hear when he tells me it is God's "voice" that addresses him during his time of praying? I became increasingly precise in my questions: "Avram, is it your dad's voice you hear, or the rabbi's, or your own? I mean, do you actually hear God's voice?" I thought I knew what he meant when he talked of God's "voice," but I had enough confidence in our friendship, its give-and-take, to go through this kind of close analysis, and I thought it was necessary for me to do so—because it is important, as Avram himself has told me, that we separate our own ideas (and wishes and concerns) from God's.

Avram could be good at clarifying. Here are some of his efforts in that direction, which I garnered from several talks: "When I pray to God, it's not like I'm talking with my friends. No, it's not the same as being with my dad or mom. They have told me to talk "special" when I speak to Him, God, and I try to do that. I bow my head; I lower my voice; I close my eyes. I say my prayers [in Hebrew]. I wait a while; then I ask Him for His help. I mention some people who are sick. I mention some people I've seen on the TV who need help. I try to give Him a report—[something] like that.

"I hear Him saying that I should work hard, and do my share. I guess He'll do His [share] if we do ours. It's my voice; it's Dad's and Mom's; but we don't talk to each other like that. It's His voice, I guess—because it's different. Just like I don't talk any other time like I do when I pray, no one talks to me the way God does—He gets me thinking, and then I hear Him. It's not His voice—I mean, He doesn't speak to us when we pray; we speak to ourselves. But it's Him telling us what to say—to tell ourselves. Do you see what I mean?"

I nodded. I remembered a prayer I once heard Dr. Martin Luther King make in Alabama—one in which he asked God to speak to him at a time of great danger, so that he would in turn have some idea of what to say to others, who were paying him the closest of heed and who were also scared and in clear danger. "Speak to us, dear God," Dr. King implored repeatedly, "so that we can hear You, and thereby ourselves." I have those words on tape. I played them once for Avram. He smiled.

God is patient and will speak to you until you get the message. Look for patterns in the things that people say to you, even in casual conversation. For example, are you so busy that your friends keep saying to you, one after another, things like, "We used to have such a wonderful time together before you became so involved," or "You're never home!" Do your grandchildren complain that they never get to stay overnight any more? Perhaps you are so busy doing things for people that you don't have time to just "be with" those who are dearest to you. Again, everyone's situation is different. Just keep looking at the patterns of the comments.

One word of caution. The fact that many people are saying the same thing to you doesn't necessarily mean that God is trying to get through. Again, it's the flash of recognition, the intuition of the truth of the message that feels "right" (or even very uncomfortable, but true) to you that makes the difference.

Friendship

I considered putting friendship as a way of coming into the presence of God in the previous category, "Other People," but decided that friendships were too special to be included there. Friendships are so important that without them people often do not want to go on living. When I ask people at workshops whether they would like to live to be 115, most often they say no and cite the death of all of their friends as one of the major reasons why they would not want those extra years.

When describing their relationship with God, very many devout people speak of God as their "best friend." When I ask what a friend is, most answer "Someone who accepts you as you are, someone you can just be yourself with." The hymn "Just as I Am" comes to mind when I hear that.

So friendships can be a precursor of our relationship with God. Sometimes they actually teach us how to be comfortable, how to be ourselves with God! Sometimes they emerge from our relationship with God.

In friendship two people can be present to one another in a freedom of giving that does not exist in any other relationship.

There is mutual understanding, a give-and-take of sharing and listening, an ever-deepening revelation and acceptance of one's innermost self. Unlike the relationship with one's spouse or children or other relatives with whom there are legal and covenantal interactions, the relationship that is friendship is total gift. One doesn't have to remain a friend. One does not have to live the daily routines of cooking, cleaning, and fixing with a friend. There are no legal obligations. There is rarely sexual passion that interferes with friendship, although passion can evolve from friendship—and many happy marriage partners were originally good friends.

When I shared with people the proposed title of this book, some said in dismay, "Oh, no. I don't want to think about having a love affair with God. God is my friend. That's as far as it goes. I'm not comfortable with the lover stuff." That's fine. Perhaps friendships for these people have been far more real, intimate, and life-enhancing than their so-called "love" relationships. As such, they point to a way of being with God and a way of letting God be present to them.

Ordinary friendship with other men and women is a tremendous gift, a special light in the world. But there is another kind of friendship, a spiritual friendship, which can be the very special food of human life. I spoke of it briefly when I told of the friends with whom I meditate and our "feeding" on each other. Some people call this type of friendship "fellowship," but I think the word has been overused and misunderstood. (Especially when every church basement is now called the "Fellowship Hall.") The Quaker Thomas R. Kelly has wonderful words with which to speak of this very different kind of friendship, which he calls the "Holy Fellowship" and the "Blessed Community." Kelly talks about the depth and intensity as well as the breadth of friendship that often emerges when two or more people who are in love with God encounter one another. He says that these people recognize one another almost instantly and bond quickly. Normal barriers of socio-economic status, age, gender, education, work, and even geographical location seem to dissolve. There is an immediacy of presence to one another that each experiences as the presence of

God in the other. It is as though they were each Christ-gift to the other, and they are consciously aware of this. Roger and Mary, the two people from the retirement home I mentioned in an earlier chapter, are good examples of this kind of spiritual friendship.

Kelly goes on to discuss an even deeper sense of spiritual relatedness, which he calls the Blessed Community. This is a community of the heart, one in which you carry within your mind and heart one or more very special people. These may be relatives, friends, or even people you have never met, but with whom you feel some kind of spiritual kinship. You feel that you have a special link with them, as though God has given them to you to keep constantly and lovingly in your heart. You are to shelter them, pray for them, cherish them, think about them. You carry them around with you as though you were pregnant with them, nourishing them with your whole body, mind, and soul. You may choose to let these people know who they are. Sometimes they will never know how important they really are, even though they know they are special to you. At other times, they will be fully conscious of being part of your "blessed community" because you are part of theirs. The mutual awareness of this kind of spiritual friendship is a gift of love that is one of the greatest joys we can experience on earth. I truly believe it is what Jesus wanted us all to learn how to experience when he tried to teach us how to love one another. In Kelly's words:

> Within the wider Fellowship emerges the special circle of a few on whom, for each of us, a particular emphasis of nearness has fallen. These are our special gift and task. These we "carry" by inward, wordless prayer. Two people, three people, ten people may be in living touch with one another through Him who underlies their separate lives. This is an astounding experience, which I can only describe but cannot explain in the language of science. . . . We know that these souls are with us, lifting their lives and ours continuously to God and opening themselves, with us, in steady and humble obedience to Him. It is as if the boundaries of our self were enlarged, as if we were within them and as if they were within us. Their strength, given to them by God, becomes our strength,

and our joy, given to us by God, becomes their joy. In confidence
and love we live together in Him.

Thomas R. Kelly, *A Testament of Devotion*

I like to think that this kind of friendship may transcend
death. One of my own special friends, Sr. Paulanne Diebold, a
Catholic Sister of Mercy, has a number of people in this category
of friends. But perhaps her most special friend, a true member of
her blessed community, is an elderly woman named Benita, who
died recently. Benita lived in the retirement home where Sr.
Paulanne was in charge of pastoral care. From the time of Benita's
first days in the home they "hit it off" in a way that Paulanne did
not experience with the other residents, many of whom she was
very fond and who were also fond of her. Benita always shrugged
off her own aches and pains and wanted to know how Paulanne (or
anyone who came to her room to visit) was doing. She was never
interested in talking about herself but was always ready to listen to
the joys and pains of others. Over a period of six years she and
Paulanne became fast friends. Paulanne often told her how much
better she felt after even a few minutes in Benita's presence.

One day, about a year before Benita's death, Paulanne and
she had a long talk about their friendship and about the life with
God that they shared, and how dearly they loved one another.
They both knew that each day of their friendship was precious, for
Benita was not in good health. Paulanne was sad thinking about
the loss of Benita. She decided to ask a favor of her. "Benita," she
said, "You and I both know that you will probably die before I do.
I have one thing to ask of you, one special favor. When you get to
heaven, will you keep me as your friend—adopt me as a special
project to pray for and keep watch over—like you would your own
children?" She felt a little odd asking for such a thing, but Benita
was extraordinarily delighted and promised to do so. When Benita
did die months later, easing the pain of her loss was the belief
Paulanne held that Benita was still with her in a spiritual way. She
carries Benita in her heart and will till the end of her days. And she
derives much joy from her belief that she is held dearly in Benita's

spiritual heart. This is the poem Paulanne wrote a few days after Benita's funeral:

Tribute to Benita Schlich

Benita,

The difference you have made!

Like a great old oak tree,
    roots reaching deep
        into the richness of life—
    branches spreading wide,
        offering shelter and refreshment,
        protection from storm,
        a hideaway and playground.

Precious memories!

My friend, rocking gently,
    offering a listening heart,
    reflecting of life experiences,
    sharing of wisdom gained from
    failures and successes,
    joys and sorrows,
  viewed with eyes of Faith.

Whole and holy,
    warmth radiating
    and sparkling eyes revealing
        the Spirit of Love and Life
        dwelling within.

Years of living and praying
    have produced this profound perspective
    of one who has grown
    in wisdom and age and grace.

Again, such depth of friendship is what Christ was talking about when he urged us to love one another. In this kind of friend love we find God, ourselves, and one another. And we have a good time, too!

Life Events

Another way to become aware of God within is to look closely at the way God has acted in your life throughout your entire life span. This is called "life review" by gerontologists, and it is an extremely important activity to be engaged in in later life. It provides you with a chance to integrate the disparate events of your life, to tie up the threads, so you can make a meaningful whole out of them. It enables you to tell the story of your life.

Telling the story of our lives is one of the most important activities of the later years. It reminds us that we are still emerging, growing people. It shows us how we have changed and how we have been transformed. In addition, it keeps us in connectedness with the community of people who are growing right along with us. It allows us to witness to the gifts that we have been given. Perhaps even more important, it keeps us "grounded" in our own existence. What does this mean?

Older people whose "families of origin" are no longer living experience a need to tell their life stories. Their parents are no longer living; they have lost the sisters and brothers who shared early family experiences. Their early childhood friends have died. There is no longer anyone living who knew them as children. This state of being can be very lonely; it feels as though you are truly an orphan in a world where no one particularly cares about who you are and how you came to be. One reason why older persons cling so strongly to material possessions (like the lady in Chapter 4) is that these things connect them with the past and ground them in reality.

For people in long-term care facilities even the reminders of the past that personal possessions can be are no longer available. These people experience orphanhood most severely. In the busyness of everyday nursing home life, there is rarely time for staff to spend listening to life stories. Often, when people try to share their stories with staff or even with one another, they are shut off due to lack of time or little interest. It is hard to remember that our own personal stories are far more interesting to ourselves that they are to one another. Many facilities have instituted the life review exercise, to enable older adults to tell their stories in a group setting. However, more often than not, this is done for therapeutic and activity purposes; few people are really interested. Very often, when attending to the cries of confused elderly, one will hear them plead, "I want to go home, please take me home." Invariably a staff person will respond with, "Now Mrs. Jones you *are* home. This is where you live," to which the older person will say "No, I don't. Take me home." The home they want to go to is the home where Mommy and Daddy live, the home of their childhood, the home where they were known. The home where they were called by name.

So life review allows us to be grounded, to be at home in our lives in a certain time and in a particular place and to share, if we so choose, our life homes with others. It is not preoccupation with the past, but a stabilization in the security of the past so that we can go beyond to embrace the future.

In addition to keeping us connected with early family life and personal identity, the time spent in review of our lives provides us with an opportunity to examine the ways in which we have been in and out of contact with God throughout the years. God has called each one of us by name from birth. How have we responded? Have there been patterns to our response? From the vantage point of many years and many experiences, we are able to see how God has touched our lives over and over again. We can see how often we have been invited to ever-deepening relationship. We can see how a call that occurred forty years ago may have just come to fruition. It gives us the long view of things. We can finally "see the forest for the trees." My friend, Episcopal chaplain Georgine Buckwalter, calls this process "taking a look at our personal salvation history." She advises older adults to take a look at their lives from earliest memory to the present, searching for patterns of God's intervention. This is a good way to reaffirm the gifts we have been given. It also gives us an opportunity to take a new look at negative experiences so that we can either redefine them or forgive ourselves and others for them. It gives us a chance to savor and appreciate the positive experiences even more.

Finally, we become aware that the one who is most interested in our lives is God. No one else but we ourselves can be as interested, because each person has his or her own story to attend to. We can share our selves through our stories, but to expect the sharing to be total is unrealistic. Your life history is ultimately a secret you share with the family of the Trinity. The Father, Son, and Spirit are the ones who called you into being and have kept you there. There is no person on earth who is more interested in the events of your life and what you have done with them than the Three Persons. So reminisce with them. Enter into conversation. Be grateful for the gifts. Complain about those you didn't like too well. Be in relationship. And you will find that your story is not over; your life continues to grow, minute by minute, in richness and meaning and love.

One activity that many people use to help them to do life review is keeping a journal. This is done in different ways. The simplest is to get a notebook and record thoughts and feelings that have affected you in some way. Things you have thought of, products of your own reflection, and things that you have read. This process keeps you in contact with what you value over time. Another journaling exercise is to have a dialogue with God. Just let God speak to you through your pen or pencil. Write down whatever you want to say. Then respond back to God. It is amazing to me what guidance can come from this kind of dialogue, which really is a form of prayer.

Music

Music, secular as well as sacred, can bring many of us into the presence of God very quickly and powerfully. Music affects the limbic system of the brain, the center that has control over all of our feelings. Since I hinted earlier that the potential for experiencing the divine is also brain-centered, I am suggesting here (with absolutely no scientific evidence) that the two areas of the brain are functionally connected. This means merely that music affects the limbic system, which in turn affects the temporal cortex, a section which seems to be sensitive to the spiritual. Although this connection is conjecture, it is interesting to ponder, and it substantiates what we already know—that we are "fearfully and wonderfully made" (Psalm 139).

I have already shared with you the spiritual significance three popular songs had for me in my early life. Other types of music have also served to calm me, energize me, or actually bring me into the realm of the transcendent. Think about the role music plays in your spiritual life. What kind of music moves you to tears? What makes you joyful, hopeful, peaceful, repentant, happy? What kind of music draws you into yourself? What pulls you out of yourself?

My very favorite hymn in the new *United Methodist Hymnal* is #184, "Of the Father's Love Begotten," the words of which were originally the *Divinum Mysterium,* with music being the eleventh century *Sanctus* trope. If you don't have a hymnal nearby, the words are:

> Of the Father's love begotten, ere the worlds began to be,
> he is Alpha and Omega, he the source, the ending
> he of the things that are, that have been and that
> future years shall see, evermore and evermore.

> Christ, to thee with God the Father, and, O Holy Ghost,
> to thee, hymn and chant and high thanksgiving,
> and unwearied praises be:
> honor, glory and dominion, and eternal victory,
> evermore and evermore.

I hear this hymn in my mind almost all the time. I sing it to myself. I sing it out loud, mostly in the morning shower (so as to drown out offense to Ron's ears—my voice is terrible). I don't remember most of the words, but I hold in my heart their meaning and a few emerge from the verses now and then. I sometimes wake up in the middle of the night with the sound of the hymn in my head, and it is like a lullaby. It is a form of wordless prayer.

If you don't have a favorite hymn, search for your very own, the one whose music and words speak as a love song or a lullaby from you to your God within. Then hum it, sing it—out loud or to yourself. Let it become part of the fabric of your being. After a while it will take on a life of its own and it will sing itself in your heart. This is very similar to the idea of praying the "Jesus Prayer" ("Lord Jesus Christ, Son of God, have mercy on me, a sinner"), only instead of just words, you pray always in words and melody. Then just melody. Just a few bars of the melody, sung when you are stressed or feeling out of touch with God, will bring you back to your center where you are in conscious connection with God.

Some of our strongest experiences of God occur in our early childhood. If this is the case with you, these experiences may have been connected with hymns that were popular in our churches at the time. Go back over old hymnals to find those melodies and words which spoke to your heart when you were a child. Psychiatrist Oliver Sacks, author of *Awakenings* and *The Man Who Mistook His Wife for a Hat*, talks about the power of church music to evoke memories and to orient one in place and time, even in people with advanced organic memory losses such as Alzheimer's disease.

Other kinds of music may be more important to you. Classical pieces have enormous power to evoke spiritual feelings and remind us of God. Even jazz, which was one of Merton's favorite forms of music, can do this for some. It is dependent on your taste. Whatever you like is fine. There is no right or wrong, nothing that is more or less appropriate. One older woman friend of mine tells me that she sings some of the 1930s and 40s "big band" love songs to God. They bring her into the presence of God more effectively than do hymns. How about the love song from *West Side Story*— "One Hand, One Heart"? Some hymns couldn't come as close as this to being prayer. So try experimenting with music as a medium for prayer—it may quicken your spirit more than any other way of being with God.

Nature

For many of us, especially as we age, nature is not only where God speaks to us—nature comes very close to embodying God. The Spanish mystic/poet John of the Cross writes, in his poem "The Spiritual Canticle":

> My Beloved is the mountains,
> And lonely wooded valleys,
> Strange islands,
> And resounding rivers,
> The whistling of love-stirring breezes,
>
> The tranquil night
> At the time of the rising dawn,
> Silent music,
> Sounding solitude,
> The supper that refreshes, and deepens love.

Ron and I spent a week of summer vacation camping at Lac La Croix in the Boundary Waters Canoe Area between Minnesota and Canada. These stanzas kept going round and round in my head as we paddled past landscape that looked just like this description. It was an intense time for me, just before I started writing this book, and the presence of God in nature was palpable—consoling, awe-inspiring, frightening, and irresistible, all at once.

In addition to being aware of the presence of God in nature, the feeling of unity with all natural things can become very strong as we age. The woman who was arrested for trying to protect an ancient redwood tree in California is an example of this progression from the love of the beauty of nature to active stewardship of creation.

You may find yourself actually becoming maternal towards nature and the little things of nature. Caring for a cat, a dog, a bird—anything alive—can gift you with a morsel of the love of God. During the depression I experienced after my accident the only things that could evoke in me any feeling other than hopelessness and agitation were the two stray cats that just showed up at our doorstep a few days before Christmas. They drew out of me feelings of affection and joy I hadn't felt in months. The act of petting them comforted me in a way nothing else could. We were being inundated with mice at the time (a good part of the depression, I'll bet), and the cats wouldn't leave. So we kept them both and named them Spike and Sheba, and they continue to be a source of great joy and lessons on leisurely living (and rodent-free existence). Our veterinarian friend Rich Eilers (Libby's dad) has as his primary clientele older adults and their pets. He speaks over and over of the intensity of the bond of love that exists between humans and their pets. He considers this relationship a sacred one and believes that some people are actually kept alive emotionally (and thus, physiologically) by their companion animals. Perhaps this is because their pets are the only remaining living things that are dependent on their owners' love for their very lives and well-being.

Your garden of flowers or vegetables can be enough to make you want to get out of bed in the morning in a way that nothing else does. I recently had a conversation with the son of a woman who is considering moving to a retirement facility. He is not sure she will do well, because he can't find one that has a garden his mother can work in. He said, "I visited her yesterday and she was very depressed. But then she took me out to her garden, to show me her roses and tomatoes, and she came alive again. She seemed to have more energy and even her eyes looked livelier. She lives for her yard, for growing things and giving them away to everyone who will take them. I'm afraid of what would happen to her if she couldn't dig in the soil and grow things."

There are many things we can do to nurture the gift of God's presence to us. I have listed just a few of the ones that, through the centuries, have proven to many, many people "openings" to God within and without. Try some, or all, of these ways of being with God. Try others that have not been discussed here. Experiment.

Keep in mind that God is reaching out to you constantly from deep within yourself. At some point, God will break through. The relationship will become deeper and more wonderful every day.

12

❦

FINAL SUFFERINGS: ENTERING INTO THE PASSION OF CHRIST

I believe nothing can happen that will outweigh the supreme advantage of knowing Christ Jesus my Lord. For him I have accepted the loss of everything, and I look on everything as so much rubbish if only I can have Christ and be given a place in him . . . All I want is to know Christ and the power of his resurrection and to share his sufferings by reproducing the pattern of his death.

Philippians 3:8, 10

SURPRISINGLY, AND WITHOUT PRIOR INTENT (my body always seems to take me places and my mind catches up later), I began writing this chapter on the last Saturday evening in August, sitting in a graveyard on the banks of Bear Creek, a lovely, rock-ledged stream which meanders throughout Grayson County and encircles like a mother's arm the graveyard in which I have recently chosen to be buried. This cemetery is very old and tiny, with worn and broken tombstones dating back as far as the early 1800's. It is filled with strong, no-nonsense, old Kentucky family names like Higdon and Mattingly and Mudd. Like the churchyards in Great Britain, the white gravestones are clustered right in front of the church, as children around their mother's skirt, seeking comfort and protection. When the congregation is ready to leave the church, and the double doors are opened at the end of the service, the stark panorama confronts you with the last things, final sufferings and the promise of ultimate peace and love. All at once.

It is enough to take your breath away. (Hopefully not yet permanently.) These long-deceased members of the body of Christ belong to St. Augustine Church in Grayson Springs, Kentucky. The monument closest to me has an inscription, chiseled in marble in 1882, in memory of one James B. Milliner, born on April 20, 1832. It warns:

Remember man as you pass by
As you are now so once was I
As I am now so you must be
Prepare for death and pray for me.

This blunt verse reminds me in no uncertain terms that someday, sooner or later, my own gravestone will be dotting this hill and other people, not I, will be driving past for a weekend of play at Nolin Lake. It also reminds me that between this late-summer evening and the morning of my burial lies a future that will hold increasing instances of suffering, for I am now forty-five and have lived beyond the mid-point of my expected life span.

As a clinical gerontologist I am confronted daily with the ravages as well as the triumphs of the aging process. For years I have spoken and written grandly and often superficially of the potential triumphs of aging; let me now speak honestly of the negative parts of advancing age. You do not need to be a gerontologist or an old person to realize that with advancing age come changes, especially deterioration of the body and mind. Our lavishly gifted bodies begin to wear out in mid-life, or they change in such a way that they no longer work for the welfare of the entire body. The mutation of normal cells into cancer cells is an example of this.

Our society fears, dreads, and abhors the aging process because it is accompanied—due to the mindset that embraces greed rather than gift—by many "bad" things. Even though I study aging daily and try to focus on the positive aspects of the aging process, I am not exempt from my own fears about aging. Here is a laundry list—not in any order of priority—of all the things I (and most other people in today's society) fear about aging.

I fear most:

♦ loss of my ability to go where and when I want to go
♦ loss of eyesight with inability to see the Milky Way and the daily newspaper
♦ loss of hearing with inability to carry on the conversation of friendship and experience Beethoven's Seventh Symphony
♦ loss of my husband Ron's protective mothering and his warm and strong body by my side—and most of all, his bizarre sense of humor (which, as he reminds me, he has to have in order to be able to live with me)
♦ loss of privacy
♦ loss of a cabin by the lake, and the canoe that lives with it
♦ loss of animal friends (including one tiny field mouse)
♦ loss of my "soul" friends to death and relocation
♦ loss of a car, my constant hermitage on wheels since the age of 16 (not the same car)
♦ loss of meaningful conversation and the "meeting of the minds" with interesting men
♦ loss of the comfort and support and friendship of both women and men
♦ loss of interest in the larger world
♦ loss of my ability to think new thoughts
♦ loss of my memory of long past and more recent events
♦ loss of my ability to give to others
♦ loss of all those who knew my childhood name
♦ loss of all who knew what my life was all about
♦ loss of those who knew my pain as well as my joy
♦ loss of financial independence
♦ loss of the sense that my life has meaning
♦ loss of my ability to be out, alone, in wild places
♦ loss of my garden
♦ loss of the pleasures of my senses, especially smell
♦ loss of my ability to work and the availability of meaningful work
♦ loss of my ability to play the piano (even though I play badly now)

I also fear:

♦   people whose paid job it is to attend to my basic physical needs
♦   total orphanhood—again
♦   being a burden to someone who doesn't love me
♦   being a burden to someone who *does* love me
♦   dying alone; dying anywhere but in the cabin
♦   being told what to do, minute by minute
♦   seeing that a person I care for and want to talk with attends to a younger, more attractive person before talking to me
♦   sharing a room with a stranger for the rest of my life
♦   knowing that my mind and skills are outdated and that even my wisdom is of no use to anyone
♦   pain so intense that I can think of nothing but my body
♦   not seeing another human being for a week at a time, except on television
♦   having to use television as church every Sunday
♦   depression, fatigue
♦   being spoken to in a condescending voice
♦   being ignored
♦   being laughed at
♦   dying slowly and painfully, cell by cell
♦   being a source of someone's impatience
♦   surviving all those I cherish
♦   misbehaving badly and embarrassing others due to ravages of Alzheimer's disease
♦   physicians who aren't interested in maintaining my old body just because it's old
♦   clergy who are no longer interested in talking to me about God and feeding my hunger for God
♦   having to give up everything that I have valued throughout my lifetime, everything that tells me and the world who I am
♦   seeing in the eyes and faces of those who are caring for me that it is time for me to allow myself to die, knowing that they are tired and have had enough suffering because of me, knowing that they want me to go—sooner rather than later
♦   feeling that even God has forsaken me

These are only some of the real sufferings that many old people experience. These are the things that those who are not yet old fear. The fear is so great that in our society two primary forces are at play in an attempt to deal with or deny the reality of suffering in later life. The first force is suicide. More older people commit suicide than young people. The highest rate of suicide in the United States is among white males between the ages of seventy-five and eighty. There is an increasing number of homicide-suicides among family members—spouses and children taking care of ill, demented, or frail elderly. There is an increase in discussion among physicians about physician-assisted suicide and euthanasia. There is also an increase in what is called "indirect life-threatening behavior" among older adults themselves. This was the topic of my doctoral dissertation. While researching it I was overwhelmed by the number of people who really don't find life worth living any longer and, while they don't feel free to commit suicide, they see nothing wrong with letting themselves deteriorate until death comes through self-neglect. This indirect behavior kills just as effectively as direct suicide. It just takes longer and increases the time of suffering.

The second force is denial of the fact that losses do occur and the body does deteriorate. We would all like to drop dead semi-suddenly, after a lifetime of health, wealth, and pleasurable, if not meaningful, activity. But most of us die rather slowly, often enough of devastating diseases. Researchers are hard at work attempting to use fetal cells to counteract the effects of both Parkinson's disease and Alzheimer's disease, with some success. However successful their attempts, this line of research appears to me to go counter to all that is truly human. It is the opening of a Pandora's Box, the end of which we will not see. It seems symptomatic of a society that is greedy for more and more life, but which is grabbing at existence rather than true life—and stealing that existence from future human beings!

How can we make sense out of all this suffering? How meaningful can life be when the body and the mind are in decline, in a state of decay and deterioration? What good is life at all? More than half a century ago psychologist Carl Jung wrote in

Modern Man in Search of a Soul that "a human being would certainly not grow to be seventy or eighty years old if this longevity had no meaning for the species to which he belongs. The afternoon of human life must also have a significance of its own and cannot be merely a pitiful appendage to life's morning."

Just what is the significance of which Jung is speaking? What I have observed of the normal aging process leads me to believe that old age is a "natural monastery." That is, the practices of self-denial that the monk, nun, or other professional religious persons undertake in order to grow into a more intimate relationship with God—the self-denial involved in fasting, relinquishing ownership of worldly goods, celibacy, chastity, simplicity of life, and solitude—are very similar to the sensory, physical, interpersonal, and material losses which we undergo naturally in our later years. Our culture has chosen to look upon these losses and decrements of old age as negative events—and so they are on the natural plane. But I believe we can also perceive these changes as natural preparation for a more intense relationship with God. It is as though God has seen fit to wean us from our greedy attachments to the world, however good the world is, in order to ready us for the Gift of Gifts—a deeper, stronger, more intimate relationship with Love itself.

One word about loss and the relationship with God in old age. Normally if the relationship with God is growing it deepens and mellows throughout the life span, so that in very old age, the experience of loving and being loved is free of concepts, thoughts, and even the ability to form mental images of Christ and his life. This can be disturbing, but it is a natural process. The task is to remain in the attitude of love, just "being there" with God, who may seem hidden, but, as we have discussed throughout this book, is ever present to us.

Feeling Forsaken by God

Another experience that is very difficult to deal with is the experience of feeling that you have lost faith in God after living a life of relative devotion. You are left with no feeling, no sense of the reality of God in your life. Prayer is impossible; all you can do is wail out in desperation to a God who seems to have forgotten all about you. There may be two reasons for this experience. The first and most common is that God is calling you to a deeper level of intimacy, and you must give up the usual, more comfortable ways of being in God's presence. John of the Cross calls this the "dark night of the soul," and it really does feel like darkness, as though all the light and love has gone from your life. When this happens, favorite prayers, scripture readings, charitable works, and so forth no longer provide a source of comfort and satisfaction, although the desire for God remains. If this is the situation, you should seek the advice of a spiritual counselor, if one is available, who knows about the inner life. If one is not available, just staying quietly in the presence of God is enough. Reading about the spiritual life may help. You will be led to God' presence. The main thing is to realize that you are not doing anything wrong; just stay where you are and do not get discouraged or feel guilty, etc. If you are depressed, seek a physician who can treat the depression; depression can make the experience of separation from God worse and can cause permanent discouragement.

The second reason for this experience of feeling forsaken by God may be physiological. A British geriatrician and a former faculty member in my department of family and community medicine once told me of a phenomenon he had observed in some older adults who had had strokes. He noticed that a significant number of his patients had lived lives of deep relationship with God before their strokes. Afterward, there appeared to be a total loss of faith, a sense that God no longer existed for them. This seeming loss of faith caused a tremendous amount of suffering for them and their families. It appears that the stroke itself may have caused the change in the person's sense of God's presence. These people had to continue their lives in very pure faith—they had to learn to live by faith alone. This is perhaps the greatest of all suffering; a true experience of Christ's cry "Why have you forsaken me?"

If Jung is correct and the afternoon of life has a meaning independent of the meaning of life at other stages of the life span, then suffering seems to be involved in some very integral way in our total development and growth toward God. Why is this so? Why can't our focus be on love and peace and the joy of our relationship with God? If Christ has already died on the cross to save us, why must we be there, too? For one answer to this I turn to a professional religious, Elizabeth Catez, known as Sister Elizabeth of the Trinity, a French Carmelite nun who lived from 1880 to 1906. She says, in her *Spiritual Testament:*

> The soul who desires to serve God night and day in his temple, by which I mean the inner sanctuary to which St. Paul refers, when he says: "This temple of God is nothing other than yourselves," that soul must resolve to share *effectively* in the Passion of her Master. She has been redeemed and in her turn must redeem others, which is why she sings on her lyre: "God forbid that I should make a display of anything except the cross of our Lord Jesus Christ"..."with Christ I hang upon the cross" and again "in this mortal frame of mine I help to pay off the debt which the afflictions of Christ still leave to be paid, for the sake of His body, the Church."
>
> "At Thy right hand stands the queen." Such is the attitude of this soul. She walks along the road to Calvary at the right hand of her King crucified, rejected and humiliated yet always so strong, so calm, so majestic, as He goes on His way to His Passion "to manifest the splendour of His grace," according to the so forcible expression of St. Paul.
>
> He wants to associate His bride with His work of redemption, and this way of sorrow which she treads seems to her the way of beatitude, not only because it leads there, but also because the Master teaches her to transcend the bitterness of suffering and find in it, like Him, her rest.
>
> Then she can serve God *day and night in His temple.* Neither exterior nor interior trials can make her leave the holy fortress in which the Master has confined her. She *no longer hungers or thirsts* for, in spite of her consuming desire for beatitude, she is satisfied with the food that was her Master's: *the will of the Father.*

She *no longer feels* "the noonday heat fall across her path" in other words: she no longer suffers from suffering. The Lamb can lead her out to the springs whose water is "life" in whatsoever way He wills, for she does not look at the paths she treads but keeps her eyes on the Shepherd who leads her.

So, in a nutshell, what does this mean? It means that the person whom God loves and who has responded by falling in love with God is invited to enter into God's work of continuing to save the world. It means realizing that you are so identified with Christ, you are so in love with his message, that you are willing to live as he lived, to die as he died. It means that you are willing to accept and redefine all of your pain and losses as an entrance into the passion of Christ. Did not Jesus tell Peter, "When you were younger, you used to fasten your own belt and to go wherever you wished. But when you grow old, you will stretch out your hands, and someone else will fasten a belt around you and take you where you do not wish to go" (John 21:18 NRSV). It means that there is now no difference between you and Christ: "It is no longer I who live, but it is Christ who lives in me." This cannot come to fullness of being unless you are willing to take on whatever cross of suffering comes your way, realizing, all the while, that *you are modeling for others, especially older persons and those watching the way in which old age can be lived, a way of being in the world. A way that recognizes and accepts suffering realistically, then transcends it.* Again—it is willingly entering into the Paschal mystery of Christ.

You will experience your share of the aging changes we all fear. If you accept them as Christ accepted the cross, wishing that they would not come to you but accepting your Father's will, you are helping to redeem the world, to put a bit more love in the world.

Acceptance of the Father's will is the key to changing one's attitude toward suffering that cannot be alleviated in some way.

One of my friends has recently experienced a very hard time in her life. Myrna has been ill and has had difficulty with her children and with her work, all within just a few months. She was so frustrated one sleepless night that she wrote the following poem:

> Pain makes me tired:
> >When I eat, my mouth hurts.
> >When I walk, my ankle hurts.
> >When I sit, my back hurts.
> >When I move, my joints hurt.
>I'm tired of pain.

Then she took the time to allow God to be present to her in scripture and found these words (Isaiah 40:31):

> Those who wait for the Lord shall
> >renew their strength,
> They shall mount up with wings like eagles.
> They shall run and not be weary,
> They shall walk and not faint.

The words gave her new sight; she became aware of the transformational, redemptive value of her own suffering. She then wrote the following affirmation of her experiences:

> I'm blessed by pain:
> >The pain in my mouth makes me aware of the
> >>excess importance I place on food.
>
> >The pain in my ankle I experience now reminds
> >>me of the original pain and how much I
> >>have improved.
>
> >The pain in my back makes me aware of my posture.
>
> >The pain in the joints makes me aware of the
> >>importance of rest.
>
> >I learn from my pain.

Myrna Page

Empathy with the Pain of Others

So one of the blessings of suffering is that often there is a lesson to be learned from it. One of the things I have learned is that, to the extent that I have suffered myself I can be in union with and sometimes helpful to another person experiencing a similar type of suffering. I should have enough empathy to be able to be with someone in his or her suffering, but it seems that I do have some difficulty with my imagination; I find it hard to put myself in someone else's shoes. If I actually go through a similar experience, I never forget how it feels. Empathy requires good visualization skills or the actual experience. Fortunately, we can learn empathy—how to put ourselves in another's place—by practicing visualization.

Other experiences can lead us into a state of empathy for the pain and suffering of others. Until recently I had little genuine concern for AIDS patients. I realized AIDS is a major public health problem but didn't give much thought to the people dying of the disease; I kept my awareness of AIDS purely clinical. One night I had a dream that taught me empathy for individual AIDS patients. I dreamed that I had just learned that I was HIV-positive and had to tell my husband that I was ill with AIDS and that he was probably HIV-positive also. I can remember the fear and dread and despair before telling him and the anger directed at me after he was told. I remember the anguish of knowing that we were both probably going to die. I remember the guilt I felt at having transmitted the disease to him. I remember waking up in a cold sweat and having those feelings stay with me throughout the day. I had actually been able to feel some small portion of the emotional pain that AIDS victims endure.

Interestingly, that day the only social worker in our department gave a report on the increase in AIDS patients in the clinic and issued a plea for faculty and staff members to obtain training to counsel AIDS patients, as she could not handle them all adequately. I had to do something about the awareness the dream had caused, so I signed up and took the course. It has been a difficult experience, one that makes me very sad and that I would rather not do. But I feel compelled to do it because now I know a little bit of what it means to have AIDS. We can't always count on dreams to provide us with empathic experiences, but listening to and spending time with people suffering in all kinds of ways, and learning about these problems can make us more aware of our need to be empathic.

What about Alzheimer's disease? What can you do with that form of suffering, when your own mind fails to be available to you? One way to deal with that possibility is to dedicate yourself, to consecrate your life right now to the purposes of God, whatever may happen to you. That means if you lose your memory and your sense of self and your autonomy, think of it as a form of dying to self. It is a way of giving yourself totally to the will of God, to be used in whatever way God sees fit. If you are in your own home, taken care of by relatives, your previously-made intentional consecration will help to ensure that you are a source of spiritual gifts to your caretakers. The same may happen if you are placed in a nursing home. The important thing is that the Father's will, not yours, be done. If that is your intent, then your life has ultimate purpose, even though you will probably not be aware of it when the time comes. So I encourage you to consecrate your body and mind, in whatever shape it ends up, to the purposes of God. Once you have done that, your mind may begin to put aside the tremendous fear that the dementing diseases bring.

Taking on the Sufferings of Others

The person who is identified with Christ has a second invitation. In addition to accepting your own suffering, are you open to taking on the sufferings of others? This is what Christ did, for he had no need to suffer his own pain; he came to take on ours. The person identified or transformed into Christ, the person who has become Christ-gift is given both the opportunity and the strength to take on the suffering of others, to help ease their burden in some way.

Now this is certainly counter to our culture, for we're always looking for ways to get out of suffering. Yet Christ is offering as gift even more suffering, above and beyond what comes accidentally or in the course of life to us? Yes. Who would want that, especially at a time of life when suffering is constantly rearing its ugly head? Those who are his lovers, those who have become aware that they live in the family of the Trinity, those who know that their lives here on earth have infinite meaning, far more meaning than they ever had before. They are being invited to become co-redeemers, with Christ, of the world, just as Paul says with these words:

> It makes me happy to suffer for you, as I am suffering now, and in my own body to do what I can to make up all that has still to be undergone by Christ for the sake of his body, the Church. I became the servant of the Church when God made me responsible for delivering God's message to you.
>
> Colossians 1:24-26

In *The Three Ages of the Interior Life* Garrigou-Lagrange is quick to state that

> Nothing is wanting in the sufferings of Christ in themselves. They have an infinite and superabundant value by reason of the personality of the Word of God made man; but something is lacking in their radiation in us.

Something is lacking. What is lacking? A realization that God is the root of our being, that the Trinity lives and loves within. The realization that we share this inner life with God—that we are not isolated, but one in it. An awareness that, if it came to fruition, it could so transform us into lovers that we would finally be enabled to really love and receive love from one another as Christ so wants us to do.

How do we make up for this lack, how do we radiate to others this love? One answer offered to us is to accept, to enter into somehow, to share, to "be with" someone else's suffering; it was

Christ's final answer, his final suffering. All else that he had done—his teaching, healing, one-to-one loving didn't quite convince more than a few people who became aware of the gift he had given them. No, he needed to take on the final suffering, which was the offering of that which we all hold most dear—our lives—in order to awaken the world to his message of love. So we, as Christ-gift, in order to help transform the world in love, in order to make up for what is lacking in the suffering of Christ— everyone's awareness of his gift—are also invited to offer ourselves, body and blood, by willingly entering into the sufferings of the world.

At first glance it seems like something rather strange, something we naturally would not be inclined to do. These sufferings would be more than we could bear. Aren't we having enough trouble getting along day by day dealing with our own pain? How could we possibly enter into and bear any more suffering, any more difficulty, any more loss?

To answer this question we need to keep in mind the words of Elizabeth of the Trinity when she says that the person who accepts the invitation to work with God at this level "no longer 'feels the noonday heat fall across her path,' in other words: she no longer suffers from suffering." This person still experiences suffering, yes, but the suffering is no longer meaningless; it is transformed into the joy of working to birth love in the world together with the One this person loves. I wonder if it is what the early martyrs felt when they faced excruciating deaths?

It is as though God and the soul of the beloved child, whom God is inviting to this work for the kingdom, have engaged in a dialogue that might sound something like this:

God asks the beloved child, "What do you desire?"
The child responds:
    I desire
        no will but yours
        no love but yours to give and to receive
        no act but yours
        no desire but yours.

I desire everything and nothing.
I desire the destiny—and frustration—of my birth . . .
   the recognition that my being is you
   and nothing else.
Whatever emerges from that, let it be so,
With all of my human self's labor and apprehension.

And God asks of the beloved child:
   Are you willing to cast away what is not of me?
      Yes
   Are you willing to accept the gift of my cross, which may
   often be the only sign of love to others?
      Yes
   Will you be with me often?
      Yes
   Will you be with me when you feel I am not there?
      Yes
   Will you be with me even when you think I am a figment of
   your imagination?
      Yes
   Will you be with me when you don't feel like it—when you
   are bored with me?
      Yes
   When the other makes you feel guilty and unworthy of me?
      Yes
   Will you be with me as I dwell in other people?
      Yes
   Will you be with me in the earth and the stars—to the outer
   boundaries of the universe?
      Yes
   Will you bring others with you to be with me?
      Yes
   Will you do whatever I ask to birth love in the world?
      Yes, with your help.
   Will you be with me forever?
      Yes, if I may.

And God responds to the beloved child:
   I am your true self and you will always find yourself in me,

just as it has been from your beginning.
Your awareness of me will never cease.

You are my child,
my beloved partner.
Through our love
together we will cherish the world.
We will enable people to be with one another
in love
in the company of the Most High.

Cherishing the world. Enabling people to be with one another in the loving company of God. This is the work that Paul is talking about, the work that is accomplished by being present to God within and all around and by our willingness to suffer the pains caused by the lack of love.

Substitutional Suffering

The process by which this is done is called by some "substitutional suffering," "redemptive suffering," or the "life of reparation." Needless to say, we don't hear much about it these days. But look around you—it's going on all the time. Who is doing it? Ada, who sends cards to the lonely and pays for them out of her food money.
• The successful, wealthy, sixty-eight-year-old businessman who gave up his beautiful home to live for eight years in the nursing home with his wife who had Alzheimer's disease. • The middle-aged schoolteacher who has given up the possibility of a married life of her own to care for a retarded, blind brother. • The successful seventy-year-old film producer who sold his business at its height when he was fifty-five so he could work for the welfare of orphans in Brazil. • The aged woman who lives by herself and is confined to bed, who sees herself as a kind of hermit, a monk, and who spends her time praying for the world and offering her pain and disability for use somewhere in the kingdom. • The couple who provides a foster home for five severely disabled

children. • The couple who adopts Down's Syndrome adults. • The ninety-year-old woman in the nursing home who has vowed privately never to complain to a staff person and to be available to staff with a smile and a listening ear, no matter how badly they treat her. • The man at the retirement home who takes prayer requests and wakes himself at 2 AM every morning to spend three hours in quiet prayer for those who need God's love. • The Alzheimer's disease scientist, director of a major regional research unit, who, year after year, works a full day as a devoted manager, spends time with his family, sleeps from ten till two at home, then returns to his laboratory at 2:30 AM to do his basic, cellular research until 7 AM. Then he takes the time in the evening to speak to a small group of family caregivers about the disease. • The middle-aged priest, though celibate, who reveals publicly to the City Council that his orientation is homosexual. While he would have preferred that fact to remain private, he feels he must show support and oneness with those in the city who are hated and are being discriminated against because of their sexual orientation. • The elderly lady who allowed herself to be chained to the redwood tree and was arrested for trespassing. All of those who lay their very lives and reputations on the line for the cause of love. All cherishing the world, enabling others to enter into the experience of Love.

How does substitutional suffering help another, other than by modeling loving behavior? Can you suffer for a person even if he or she does not know about it? For an answer to this we can go to the doctrine of the body of Christ, to systems theory, and to quantum physics! Paul tells us that we are all members of the body of Christ—all of us, living and dead, are members of one body. That means that we are interconnected; what happens to one affects us all. Systems theory says essentially the same thing—that each one of us is part of a vast interconnection of systems that are constantly interacting. If you effect change in one area, there is going to be change in another. Sometimes you can predict where the change will occur; sometimes you can't.

For example, the change in a dysfunctional, alcoholic family when one member decides to get help is phenomenal. It need not be the alcoholic himself or herself who makes the first movement toward change. The spouse or child can decide to enter a support group such as Al-Anon or go into private therapy. This decision will effect a change in that family's life. The life of the alcoholic is affected, and the alcoholic's behavior begins to change, often, at first, for the worse. As the family member who goes to therapy changes, the alcoholic family member is forced to do some changing, to join Alcoholics Anonymous, go into treatment, or become an even more serious alcoholic. In either case, the entire family system has changed.

The same principle applies in quantum physics. This theory of the physical universe essentially says that all matter is interconnected in some way, even at the level of subatomic particles. Because there exist only particles of energy and space everything exists in relationship with everything else. A change or movement in one particle sets off a tremendous change in others.

The bottom line, the primary message is truly that no one is an island. We are all part of one another; we are in union with one another whether we know and experience this fact or not. The source and ground of this union is our rootedness in God. If we stay consciously grounded in God, we will very quickly and effectively be taught how to love ourselves and one another.

How is this related to substitutional suffering? It means that if you choose to enter into the sufferings of others, if you choose to bear their burden, either in active service of some kind, or through a more contemplative activity such as prayer, *you will effect change*. If your will is in union with God's will, the change you will effect will be what God desires. That is, more love will be spread out upon the earth.

Not only will you effect change; you yourself will change. In the process of suffering you will become outwardly the person you are in the eyes of God. All of your masks will fall away and you will become *real*. In the story, *The Velveteen Rabbit,* the lonely little stuffed toy rabbit had remained on the nursery shelf in the little boy's room since Christmas; the boy had played with him for two hours, then put him aside, forgotten among the expensive, showy mechanical toys who were "full of modern ideas, and pretended they were real. . . . The poor little rabbit was made to feel himself very insignificant and commonplace, and the only person who was kind to him at all was the Skin Horse." In his loneliness the Rabbit asks the Skin Horse:

"What is REAL?" asked the Rabbit one day, when they were lying side by side near the nursery fender, before Nana came to tidy the room. "Does it mean having things that buzz inside you and a stick-out handle?"

"Real isn't how you are made," said the Skin Horse. "It's a thing that happens to you. When a child loves you for a long, long time, not just to play with, but REALLY loves you, then you become Real."

"Does it hurt?" asked the Rabbit.

"Sometimes," said the Skin Horse, for he was always truthful. "When you are Real you don't mind being hurt."

"Does it happen all at once, like being wound up," he asked, "or bit by bit?"

"It doesn't happen all at once," said the Skin Horse. "You become. It takes a long time. That's why it doesn't often happen to people who break easily, or have sharp edges, or who have to be carefully kept. Generally, by the time you are Real, most of your hair has been loved off, and your eyes drop out and you get loose in the joints and very shabby. But these things don't matter at all, because once you are Real you can't be ugly, except to people who don't understand."

"I suppose you are Real?" said the Rabbit. And then he wished he had not said it, for he thought the Skin Horse might be sensitive. But the Skin Horse only smiled.

"The Boy's Uncle made me Real," he said. "That was a great many years ago; but once you are Real you can't become unreal again. It lasts for always."

The Rabbit sighed. He thought it would be a long time before this magic called Real happened to him. He longed to become Real, to know what it felt like; and yet the idea of growing shabby and losing his eyes and whiskers was rather sad. He wished he could become it without these uncomfortable things happening to him.

Margery Williams, The Velveteen Rabbit

Suffering—allowing oneself to risk being hurt for the sake of love—ultimately means growth for all involved—the one loving and the one being loved. It is integral to becoming who you are. Not only did Christ suffer and accomplish for us what he needed to do, he became who he really was in the process. Nothing else would have allowed him to become real. But even Christ wished that he could accomplish his task "without these uncomfortable things happening to him." So you must be gentle with yourself if you still do not like the idea of suffering. That is the healthiest attitude. But you must also have the courage to enter into suffering if that is the only way to witness to reality—your own and others'.

How can you take part, become a partner with God, in this work of substitutional suffering? First, as is usual with God, you must desire and ask for this work—it will never be forced upon you. Second, you should be growing daily in your oneness with God and God's desire to enliven all things with love. Third, you should talk about your desire to do this work with your own Skin Horse, a spiritual counselor or minister who knows you well. That person will help you determine if you are really ready for this work, or if you need to keep your attention on your own growth for a while longer.

Sometimes taking on the burdens of others is a way to escape looking at ourselves. We need to know ourselves to the depths, be acutely aware of our weaknesses as well as our strengths before we can undertake this work. Otherwise we might do others, as well as ourselves, unnecessary harm. Jesus himself went off into the desert for forty days and nights to prepare himself for this work, and the preparation period was certainly not easy for him. Neither is it for anyone who wants to follow him in this way. This work is not a hobby; it goes beyond the ordinary expectations of loving one's neighbor to laying down one's life for one's neighbor, and it will ultimately use you up completely. You will, eventually, in some way specially given as gift to you, die on this cross of love.

But the death of one who dies of this kind of suffering is a death of joy, a reunion with the Beloved, a breaking of the thin veil that was the only hindrance to the full realization of unity. If you die in this state you may experience great pain or abandonment—continuing to suffer for others—but you will die of ecstasy. When you are fully developed and mature; when your gestational period on this earth has come to the birth time, your Advent will end and you will be born into eternity. Your soul will leap straight into the waiting arms of the Father.

I wrote a poem sixteen years ago for Jacob, an elderly homecare client who was dying. Jacob was a rabbi—a holy man, who, from very early youth, had lived a life totally dedicated to bringing his people into the presence of God. In the short time I knew him, he affected my own life profoundly. He had suffered very much in the process of birthing others in God, including years of pain and loss of his entire family at Auschwitz. In his time of dying he was beset by fears that he hadn't served his God well enough; he could only remember what he had failed to do. Nothing could console him. He continued, even at his death, to suffer for others. His life was now the life of Ariel—the altar of the holocaust in the Temple of Solomon—for Jacob had given all to God, with no remaining morsel left to feed the rabbi in himself. There was nothing I could do to help him except provide for his physical needs. But I wrote this poem, mostly for myself, in an attempt to ease some of his anguish and my sadness. I imagined his death and that of others who enter this work of voluntary suffering for the rest of us to be something like this:

To Jacob, Dying

Suddenly

A time will come
when you will empty out
    into the universe,
Taking to your heart
    the light of ages
    now and long ago.

You will spread
    as dandelion wings
    into the vast distances
    of past and future,
And be filled
    with all the splendours
    of the heavens.

You will hear your name
    chanted through the void
    in strange and lovely languages
    inviting you to follow
    and expand;

And you will be one with them
            knowing each, in intimate communion
            as your brother
            and your lover
            and your friend.

13

GOD'S CALL IN LATER LIFE

About then, Hezekiah fell ill and was at the point of death. The prophet Isaiah son of Amoz came and said to him, 'Yahweh says this, "Put your affairs in order, for you are going to die, you will not live." Hezekiah turned his face to the wall and addressed this prayer to Yahweh, "Ah, Yahweh, remember, I beg you, that I have behaved faithfully and with sincerity of heart in your presence and done what you regard as right." And Hezekiah shed many tears.

Then the word of Yahweh came to Isaiah, "Go and say to Hezekiah, 'Yahweh, the God of your ancestor David, says this: I have heard your prayer and seen your tears. I shall cure you: in three days' time you will go up to the Temple of Yahweh. I shall add fifteen years to your life.' "

Isaiah 38:1-5 NJB

After hearing that he would receive the gift of fifteen more years, Hezekiah wrote a poem himself:

I thought: In the noon of my life
I am to depart.
At the gates of Sheol I shall be held
for the rest of my days.
I thought: I shall never see Yahweh again
in the land of the living,
I shall never see again a single one
of those who live on earth.

My home has been pulled up, and thrown away
like a shepherd's tent;
like a weaver, I have rolled up my life,
he has cut me from the loom.
From dawn to dark, you have been making an end of me;
til daybreak, I cried for help;
like a lion, he has crushed all my bones,
from dawn to dark, you have been making an end of me.
I twitter like a swallow,
I moan like a dove,
my eyes have grown dim from looking up.
Lord, I am overwhelmed, come to my help.
How can I speak and what can I say to him?
He is the one to act.
I must eke out the rest of my years
in bitterness of soul.

The Lord is over them; they live,
and everything in them lives by his spirit.
You will cure me. Restore me to life.
At once, my bitterness turns to well-being.
For you have preserved my soul
from the pit of nothingness,
you have thrust all my sins behind you.
For Sheol cannot praise you,
nor Death celebrate you;
those who go down to the pit
can hope no longer in your constancy.
The living, the living are the ones who praise you,
as I do today.
Fathers tell their sons
about your constancy.
Yahweh, come to my help
and we will make our harps resound
all the days of our life
in the Temple of Yahweh.

Isaiah 38:10-20 NJB

"The living, the living are the ones who praise you . . . We will make our harps resound all the days of our life in the Temple of Yahweh." This praise of God in the loveliness of music is the final, supreme work that Hezekiah felt he was liberated from suffering and death and called to do. This is the work he decided to do in order to creatively transform the extra time that God had given him. It's obvious that this is the one activity he enjoys the most and he is confident that God enjoys the music-making he and his friends provide.

What does Hezekiah's experience say to the older person today? What do his words mean for the person who is given the years after retirement to do with as he or she will? What response does the gift of these extra years ask of *you*? What message do you hear spoken to you in the experience and in the words of Hezekiah?

Could it mean that there is yet another gift for you to receive? What on earth else could there be!

You have accepted the Gift of Gifts. You have entered into your depths and found the God who is creativity and love and energy within you and all around you. You are learning to accept and transform your suffering into your gift. You have fallen madly in love, head-over-heels in love with Love. What could possibly be left? Still another gift. That wonderful mystic, Meister Eckhardt, assures us:

> There is no stopping place in this life—nor was there ever one for any man, no matter how far along his way he'd gone. This above all then, be ready at all times for the gifts of God, and always for new ones.

What is this gift? It is a new call, a new way of being in this world. A new vision for the later years. A new vocation.

For what purpose are you to receive this new gift? For the life of this world, in all its messiness. For the children of this world— all of them everywhere, including you. For the animals and the trees and the rocks and the air and the soil and the water of this world. For everything that needs to be mothered and fathered,

nurtured by you. For everything that exists now, has been and will
be in the future. Be assured and keep constantly in mind that you
are not yet dead, even if society—including the church—would
like to convince you that you are.

Older adults are the potential prophets of our time; most of
you just don't realize yet how needy the world is of your work to
birth love in the world.

I see four types of responses that the older person can make to
this gift—four ways of responding to the call to follow Christ, to
be in partnership with the Trinity in late life. These ways, which
are interrelated and can overlap are the ways of:
(1) "being with" prayer
(2) spiritual legacy
(3) redemptive suffering
(4) spiritual parenthood
(5) spiritual community

"Being With" Prayer

"Being with" God is not just one among many responses to the call
to follow Christ. It is what being a follower of Christ is all about.
All other activity, whatever it is, evolves and flows from this one
activity. No activity will be pure and selfless unless it flows from
such prayer. It is only by being with Christ, listening to Christ, that
we receive the courage to love and actually learn how to love the
Father, ourselves, other people, and all of creation. To follow
Christ is to spend all of our time with Christ, listening to his
instruction, receiving his love, and then acting on what we have
been given. It's as simple as that. *We cannot truly follow Christ
unless we spend time—all of our time—in his presence.* This is
why Paul told us to pray always. "Being with" God always and in
all things is constant prayer. If we are not in constant prayer we
have a strong tendency to run off in the direction of greed, the
vision of the world. We do this not only because we are weak but
also because that vision is so strong.

The primary way to follow Christ and to be in partnership with the Trinity in late life is to dedicate yourself to a life of prayer and adoration, just "being with" the Trinity within. You do not have to pray for anyone or anything in particular; just the act of spending time with God is enough. Keep in mind that the only thing that Christ ever asked for himself is that Peter, James, and John stay with him and keep awake while he was going through his excruciating agony in the Garden of Gethsemane. He didn't want or ask them to *do* anything to alleviate his pain; all he wanted was their silent, comforting, aware presence. It was so difficult for them to stay still and just *be* that they couldn't give him the one thing that he wanted.

Think of yourself as one of these disciples and try to stay awake for him. Or, think of yourself as who you really are, a special friend, a partner of Christ who still needs your presence to enable him to keep pouring love into the hearts of humankind. Be his companion, his helpmate, his confidante, his beloved child, his joy, the bearer of his grief; be the one who is his "soul friend." He needs this kind of love from you—perhaps now more than ever before in history. Do not let yourself doubt the value of this prayer.

While we are all called to "be with" God constantly, this way as a deliberate vocation is particularly suited to the lovers of this world, those who feel drawn to offering themselves to loving God in what is sometimes called *contemplation*. Often, these people are too gentle to be living and competing in the "dog-eat-dog" world out there and get badly battered when they try. Their place is by Christ's side, offering the shelter of companionship. This does not mean they are weak and cannot compete; it means that they are "special friends," and that their vocation is to special friendship with a God who needs their presence as much as they need God's.

This way of adoration is also suited to those who feel badly that they cannot be out there in the world "doing something useful," active, recognizable to all. Those people confined to bed in nursing homes and in their own homes. Those people so wracked by pain that they can no longer be with others for very long. Those people who can no longer hear or see. Those people for whom society has no place or function. These are the exiles, these are the hidden ones who can now become company for Christ, who are finally free to spend all their time and remaining energy with him, supporting him, loving him. He needs this: whether we want to realize it or not, God does seem to need us, God intensely desires our love. We can give to Christ what Peter, James, and John could not—just "being with" him and being aware of his goodness and love.

Intercessory prayer is another form of this way of following Christ. In intercessory prayer we bring all the needs, the pains, the sorrows of the world to the center of the Trinity. No one knows how, but God does respond to prayer, and we have certainly been promised that response by Christ. Praying for the well-being of the body of Christ is work that takes dedicated time and consecrated energy. The people who have these elements to the greatest extent are monks, cloistered nuns, and the elderly, especially those who cannot be active—those who are ill or are taking care of frail older adults. The body of Christ needs this prayer—there are so few monks and nuns; it's up to the older person to heed the call to a life dedicated to prayer. Very few others will.

Just a personal pondering—I wonder if the fate of the world could rest on the prayer life of its elders?

Spiritual Legacy

One response to the call to be in partnership with the Trinity in late life is that of finding and leaving one's spiritual legacy. It is easy to become preoccupied with your will and your estate as you age. How preoccupied are you with your spiritual estate? What is it that you want to leave behind for the welfare of all God's family when you die? What is unique and special to you? What uses your skills, talents and gifts to their fullest, as music-making did Hezekiah?

Many people, when I ask this question, respond with "my children." Children don't "count" as spiritual legacy for they were the gift of your youthful years. But involvement with your grandchildren could well be your spiritual legacy. You have the opportunity to be very influential in their growth and development of values, far more so than you realize. You and no one else will teach them how to age throughout the life span. You will model healthy, vital aging. You will be the one responsible for allaying their fears about their own aging process. You alone are the storyteller of the family—the one who carries the history and makes the meanings from the vantage point of years. (Research has shown that the medical students who choose to specialize in geriatrics are primarily those who have had a close relationship with a vitally involved and interesting grandparent. I would venture to say that these grandparents were not even aware of the ways they were influencing these future doctors.)

A more formal response would be involvement in volunteer work, such as delivering meals to shut-ins, reading to the blind, offering respite care to families with Alzheimer's disease victims, being a foster grandparent—any kind of volunteer service. The opportunities are countless; there is a way for every interest, every type of personality. You must look for an opportunity to serve, keeping in mind that only you can give what you have been given, and your gifts are a unique manifestation of the blessings of God in this world.

Another, more hidden way, is to become someone who can "be with" others in their pain and suffering and in their joy. So few of us are able to engage in this kind of presence to one another. We are more comfortable with "doing" something for one another; if we can't do something active, very often we will avoid the person. But what most of us really yearn for is someone who will listen, really listen to us. Someone who will be silent but fully present to us. When my father was dying of cancer, many of even his closest friends failed to come to see him. People we would never have dreamed would abandon him did. People whom we would never have predicted would start visiting began to come regularly. It was the strangest phenomenon. Those visits kept him involved with life, kept him part of the human community, and validated his worth as a person far more than anything anyone could have "done" for him. For there was simply nothing to do. "Being with" was the only activity left.

The ability to be with another in quiet and silence is a natural gift which some people have. However, it can be learned, because it is both a skill and a value, even if you don't have an ounce of it. If you do value it enough you can learn the skill fairly easily. There are a number of books on the market which deal with listening and communication skills. Classes are taught on this topic alone. Pick up a book or try a class. Not only will development of the gift of "being with" enable you to help others and leave your spiritual legacy in this way, you'll find yourself increasingly able to be with your own self and God within your self. The work for peace and justice is another way to leave one's spiritual legacy.

Redemptive Suffering

I have talked at great length of substitutional suffering and the life of reparation, so I won't expand on it here. It is a very special vocation and certainly not one desired by all. Yet it offers a perfect opportunity for spiritual growth and dedication for those people who are victims of disease, pain, and disability. It is a way to transform an apparently negative life experience into a means by which your own and others' welfare can be affected in a positive way.

Spiritual Parenthood

Spiritual parenthood is a vocation that can be a very special call of later life; it actually requires the wisdom gleaned from a long lifetime of prayer, suffering, reflecting, acting, and being with God. In the vocation of spiritual parenthood, you work in partnership with Christ to birth in others the awareness of the presence of God in their lives. I am sure you have done this in one way or another nearly all of your life. You engaged in spiritual parenthood when you first introduced your own children to God— when you taught them their first prayers, when you had them baptized, when you taught them loving behavior, and when you answered their questions about God. You engaged in spiritual parenthood when you taught Sunday School and at any time, formally or informally, that you enabled another person to come to the awareness of God. You engaged in spiritual parenthood every time you witnessed to the love of God by the way you lived your life.

How can you enter intentionally into spiritual parenthood as a vocation, a calling in later life? The first step is to become a good listener. People all around you, of every age, are needing a listening ear. They are desperate to tell their stories and to try to make some sense of their lives. Teenagers are in particular need, as are people in the meaning crisis of middle age. They need a person who is willing and able to be quiet, to be with them in silence, just listening. This listening is a most profound way of loving, a way of allowing God to be with them through you in that moment. As you listen, you will hear, at some point, the cry for God. At this time only, and not until this time, can you share the God within you with this person.

That sharing can take many forms. It might be a prayer together. It might be an invitation to join you in a church service. It might be the lending of a book you think might help. It might be the introduction of that person to a minister or someone more competent than you to lead this person more formally and intentionally to God. This vocation requires the utmost flexibility and some reticence, combined with a sense of timing. This vocation requires that you think of yourself perhaps more as a midwife or an obstetrician than an actual parent. God is the parent; you assist with the pregnancy and the birth, providing support, encouragement, and the right information at the right time, depending on the month of gestation. You can take no credit for the final product; it is not your legacy. You have merely allowed God to give love through you to one more person, enabling that person to see only God. If the person sees primarily you, you have not done your job well enough.

A more formal way to respond to this vocation is to enter a seminary program of training in pastoral care, spiritual direction, and/or spiritual companioning. Spiritual companioning programs are being developed around the country. These are usually one- to two-year training programs, not necessarily based in seminaries, which teach lay people how to listen, to counsel, and to discern the way God is acting in their lives and in the lives of others. They are not meant to be professional training; they recognize the particular vocation to spiritual parenthood and offer skills by which people can use their gifts in response to this vocation. The development of these programs does not mean that you cannot be a spiritual parent without training. However, in the complexity of this modern day it helps to know what is going on with a person psychologically as well as spiritually. But do not hold back from the practice of this vocation if you are called to it. The training will come, even if it is primarily through your own reflective reading.

A word of caution. Spiritual parenthood can be an "ego trip," a temptation to self-aggrandizement. One can easily develop what the psychologists call a "Messiah Complex," whereby your sense of self-importance becomes paramount and you exert power and control over another in an attempt to help him or her. Be aware of this temptation; when acted upon it can do great harm to yourself and others.

Spiritual parenthood is also the loneliest of all vocations, in terms of relationships with others, because the people you have helped to birth must go on to respond to their own unique calling. They leave you, just as grown children must leave the comfort and security of their parents. They must be free to become adult, and in that process of growth they may reject you. They may never come back. Because of the potential for your attachment to them (which is only natural—they are your spiritual children, after all, and you may actually feel closer to them than to your own biological children who may not share your relationship with God) and due to a hesitancy to let them go, which is also natural, you must practice a form of detachment called spiritual celibacy. This is constant awareness that you must be very careful not to cling to your spiritual children, not to keep them with you for your own enjoyment, your own companionship. They must never be used to fill a void in your life, to ease your loneliness. Be ever mindful that your joy must always remain solely in your solitary groundedness in God, your knowledge that in your partnership with God you are helping to give birth to love in the world. This is the only reason for responding to this call. Find your ongoing spiritual comfort and companionship in those who share the way with you, not in your spiritual children.

Spiritual Community

One way to alleviate the loneliness of later life and to find human comfort and spiritual companionship is through community. Another vocation of later life may be the call to live in spiritual community. Why must we live alone? Why must we live in proprietary nursing homes in which other people are making huge profits on our monthly payments? Are we not called to experience the joys, the support, the encouragement that comes from sharing with one another at the deepest level?

I quoted earlier from the Quaker, Thomas Kelly. Remember his words about the joys of "Holy Fellowship and Blessed Community"? He spoke of the intimacy that develops between and among people when, grounded in the love of Christ, they encounter one another and recognize the Christ within. There is no human joy, no oneness, no delight of companionship—even sexual unity—which can compare with this communion, which is communion in the body of Christ. It is energizing, inspiring, vitalizing; it is truly being in love and sharing that love. Sometimes we experience this at a meaningful liturgy; sometimes in the fellowship of a Sunday school class or a Circle. But it quickly leaves when the occasion is over and we are left nostalgic, on the alert for the next occasion of communion.

Why can't we arrange our lives so that opportunity for this fellowship, this communion of souls, is ongoing? What I'd like to see in every congregation is the development of small groups of older adults—no more than ten or twelve—that gather together intentionally to share their faith and to grow in it. It would be similar to the Holy Clubs that John and Charles Wesley founded when they were at the university. But these groups would be filled with older adults who desire to support and encourage one another in their growth in God.

These groups could develop by meeting weekly at church or in one another's homes for prayer, faith sharing, and some kind of small meal. The focus would be on the nurturing of the life of prayer, as this inner work is the primary means by which individuals deepen their own relationship with God and can recognize God in others. Perhaps an older, retired minister could be the spiritual guide, counselor, or director (whatever word you like best) for the group. This would be different from Sunday school, although it could arise out of a Sunday school class. The difference is in the level of commitment to one another. People in this spiritual community would make some commitment to the spiritual growth of one another until death. They would become spiritual family, soul friends for one another.

As time went on and members of these groups developed spiritual and emotional intimacy with one another, they might want to commit to sharing living space or to living independently yet close by one another. This would be an alternative to moving to a retirement community. The church to which they belong could support them spiritually; they might want to pool some financial resources to enable one another to live simply. This type of community, similar to the early Christian communities, would demonstrate to the world that it need not fear the loneliness, the deprivation, and the disability of old age. There would be friends of the soul to support one another through old age unto death. All in the shadow of the church steeple.

There are all kinds of ways this type of community can be envisioned and implemented. They can occur in church communities and even among people already living in nursing homes. Perhaps what we first need are people who will study the way community is developed, then go out to churches to talk about the development of small Christian communities for the aged. Perhaps this is your vocation?

It is now time for you to receive your new gift. It is time for you to listen and to hear the gift of God's call, for God is calling you by name, calling you as Abraham and Sarah were called in their very late life. Calling you to a new sense of meaning. Calling you to partnership with the Trinity; calling you to a new life of creative loving; calling you to receive the passionate energy that is the newborn, the issue of the marriage of the Creator and the Lover.

You, beloved child of age and of this age, are called to be birthed again as Christ-gift to creation. Nothing else will ease the painful longings of your heart. Nothing else will ease the heartaches of this world.

I end these pages with the prayer of Paul for the Ephesians, which he prayed also for you:

This, then, is what I pray, kneeling before the Father, from whom every family, whether spiritual or natural, takes its name:

Out of his infinite glory, may he give you the power through his Spirit for your hidden self to grow strong, so that Christ may live in your hearts through faith, and then, planted in love and built on love, you will with all the saints have strength to grasp the breadth and the length, the height and the depth; until, knowing the love of Christ, which is beyond all knowledge, *you are filled with the utter fullness of God.*

Glory be to him whose power, working in us, can do infinitely more than we can ask or imagine; glory be to him from generation to generation in the Church and in Christ Jesus for ever and ever. Amen.

Ephesians 3:14-21

Epilogue

AN OLD MAN NAMED JOHN

IN THE FIRST CHAPTER I MENTIONED THE DIFFICULTY THAT I had in writing this book, that it took me five years to begin to write about the relationship with God in later life. In the fourth year, after the automobile accident, when the theme came to mind and I actually did try to get some words down, my anxiety level went sky high. I became depressed to the point of immobilization, and I realized that I'd better hoof it to a psychotherapist for some counseling.

The depression turned out to be the source of gift, for in the course of therapy I learned many things about myself and my own barriers to the God who is "Abba," my difficulty seeing myself as a child of this constant and provident love, and my resistance to the realization that I truly do live, here and now, in the kingdom of God. So, in the course of time, I did write, and as I wrote I began to change, to forgive myself and others, and to see the events of my own life as gift; I began to be healed.

I thought I was fully healed the day I sent in the first draft of this book to the folks at the Upper Room. What joy, what relief! Yet, I had begun to see this book as my child and it was hard to send it away to be scrutinized by editors. I lived in fear and trepidation while it was being read. Then, six weeks later on October 15, Lynne called, told me the baby was fine, and that she liked it; best of all, it needed just a few minor changes. I was elated. No major revisions! No rejection of my "child"! All I had to do was sit down and retype a few things and quickly send the new version to the Upper Room. No big deal, right? WRONG!

I found that, to my great frustration, once again I could not write! What was wrong this time? The months between the completion of the book and the first of the year had been full of continuing insight into my relationship with God, especially my own sense of call to help nurture the spiritual lives of older adults. Yet when it came time to finish this book I again experienced what clinicians call "paralysis of the will." I could no longer write and, to my great distress, I could not figure out why!

It was in this conflicted state of mind that I sat in the warm sun on the beach of Nokomis (the name of Hiawatha's loving old grandmother, if I recall). I had a great need to be alone, so Ron was off on the jetty, happily fishing to his heart's content. I had brought the manuscript of this book with me, just in case I was overcome with the urge to write. All around me were people chatting about their various states of health and disease, the status of their pension funds, and the accomplishments of their grandchildren. For some reason this conversation irritated me to the nth degree. I had not come to Florida to have a busman's holiday—this is what I listened to every day at work! Get me out of here! So I picked up my chair and blanket and wandered down the beach, to a more secluded area where there were no people— just an occasional walker or shell-collector. That was better.

I swam and snorkeled, finally able to enjoy the sea-salt taste and clam-flats-at-low-tide smell of the Gulf. I then settled into my chair with a new book and a small bag of nacho corn chips, content and alone at last (except for one friendly sea-gull who settled in about five feet from me and appeared to want to preen and show himself off, then take a snooze). That's fine with me— just don't talk to me, I thought. I read and munched and snoozed a bit myself.

A while later, the bag of chips almost empty, I glanced up from my book and saw the gull looking hungrily and expectantly at me, seeming to want junk food more than fish. So, taking pity, I threw him a few chips. What a mistake! Out of nowhere came what appeared to be hundreds of seagulls, all wanting the same chip, all flying too close to the top of my head for comfort. All screeching at the top of their lungs, all apparently angry at me because I didn't have food for each and every one of them. I've never been in the middle of and the center of attraction of a flock of birds before—it was a scene right out of Alfred Hitchcock!

At this point, out of the corner of my eye I caught a glimpse of a thin old man wearing a black bathing suit and a straw hat hobbling in the sand toward me, wildly waving his arms above and all around him. *Oh no—as if birds weren't enough, I have to put up with a human being now, too! I'll just look down at my book, not make eye contact, and maybe he won't come any closer.* But he kept walking toward me, very obviously intent on making some sort of contact.

"God-dear," I growled mentally, "Did I not inform you that I am on vacation from the subject of aging and from all older people—actually, from anything that smacks of work—for this week? Don't you ever listen to your voice mail? I do not want to talk to this man. Make him go away!" God did not hear this voice mail, either, and the man finally made it to my chair. His presence and flailing arms had scattered the gulls to other parts of the beach, where they took up new positions of expectancy—watching, still waiting to be fed nacho cheese flavored corn chips.

His first words were, "If you feed them they'll never let you alone again." Oh, brother. Remind me not to offer you a corn chip, I grumbled inwardly and stuffed the bag of remaining chips under my book. Outwardly, I smiled sweetly and said, "Hello, can I help you with something?" What a hypocrite!

He laughed and replied, "You're the one who needed the help. Those things can get vicious when they fight over food. You could have been scratched. Thought I'd come over and shoo them away for ya." Put in my place. OK, I'll be friendly and hospitable for a minute or two. So we talked. For about two hours. He was very hard of hearing so we sat shoulder to shoulder for the duration of the conversation so that he could hear me with his good ear.

We exchanged names. He was John Noland, seventy eight years old, from Canada. We chatted superficially for a short time about Nova Scotia and the fishing village where he'd been born; he told me where to go and what to see in case Ron and I ever decided to vacation there. Then suddenly, and I don't remember how the subject changed, we were talking about suicide. He told me he thought the "suicide machine" developed by a physician to help people end their lives was a very good thing. He wondered if anyone in Florida had access to one. Wasn't I, as a person who worked with useless old people, in favor of suicide when they became "no good for anything?" I told him how negative I feel about it and why (if you've read this book from the front rather than starting at the end, you can deduce the reasons for my negative attitude toward suicide). We debated and wrestled verbally and emotionally for an hour: John gave situations in which he thought suicide was the best solution, and I argued why the person was still of value and an integral part of society and offered other options for help.

After listening to what John was saying for just a few minutes it was obvious to me that it was his own suicide he was trying to justify, yet he definitely did not want to talk about himself. So the whole conversation stayed on a theoretical level. I tried to assess whether he had clearly formed plans and how imminent his attempt was. He seemed to be very vague about plans for the evening and the following day. Gone was my reluctance to listen and to talk—this man was in trouble! If I had been in my clinic office there would have been plenty of intervention options available to him. The only thing I could offer now was a listening ear and engagement in conversation.

Unexpectedly he started talking about himself and brought up his fear about life after death. Then abruptly and agitatedly yet somewhat reluctantly he said, "That's religion. If we get on that subject, there'll be no end. I have to go." Realizing that I had to keep him there until I could come up with some assurance that he would not kill himself that evening I said "Oh, religion's my favorite subject. I'm even trying to write a book on spirituality and aging. See? Here it is. Why don't you stay just a little longer. Maybe you could help me with a part I'm having trouble with." I held my breath as he hesitated and deliberated. Then he sat back down and said he'd stay just a few more minutes. By this time the sun was far down in the sky over the Gulf of Mexico, and I knew we'd have to leave the beach fairly soon.

He quickly took the lead and blurted out, "I believe in God but I don't believe in Jesus Christ."

"Oh?"

"No. I believe in God because the land, sea, everything is so beautiful. God couldn't make a mistake. When they say that Christ came to save us from our sins, to me it means that God made a mistake with us and then realized he had to fix it so he arranged for his son to be murdered. I just can't go along with that—it doesn't make any sense at all!" He didn't appear to be asserting a confident statement of his current belief. Rather, he seemed to have lost something and was feeling betrayed. There was anger in his voice. And a trace of longing. And fear. And intense loneliness. I knew I needed to respond, but didn't have the slightest idea what to say. I didn't know what John needed to hear.

"Now's the time for you to answer your voice mail, dear God," I screeched into the vast recesses of my being and his being, reaching out for God's presence within us both. "How do I respond to this? What is this man really saying to me? Did he ever believe in Christ or has he always believed this way? Am I imagining his pain? If not, who is the one who has betrayed him, abandoned him—who has murdered him symbolically? Has he lost his sense of meaning? What do I say?" It was clear that John was waiting for me to say something more than "Oh."

Suddenly the content of a sermon I had heard at a service on New Year's, just a few days before, came flooding into my mind, and I shared the message with John. The scripture reading had been Galatians 4:4-7. The theme of the sermon dealt with the idea that Christ came to show us how to be human beings who were adopted children of God—how to be fully, totally, completely, and wonderfully human. How to appreciate our humanness. The emphasis was not on our shortcomings but on our potential for loving and enjoying one another and everything in creation. We don't know how to do this well enough yet; we need Christ to show us over and over how to love. We are children of the Abba-Father and, as such, we are to inherit the kingdom and everything

in it, just as Christ did. And this Abba sent his son to let us know
about our inheritance and how to receive it (or something like
that).

There was a long silence. John seemed to be processing the
words. Gradually, he became calmer. "I never thought of it that
way," he said. "That makes much more sense to me. Yes, I do like
that." With that statement he started getting up off the sand, looked
at the darkening sky, and said, "Guess I'd better go. This religion
talk could go on forever." I still didn't know how he was feeling
and how intent on suicide he was. I did know I had to give him
something to anticipate, something that gave him a future,
however small.

So I said, "And I could discuss this till the cows come
home—we're just getting started. I'll be here tomorrow. Can you
come by? We can have another good debate. Maybe you could
give me some ideas for the book—I'd like to write about meeting
you here on Nokomis beach!" He paused and I thought, he must
think I'm truly nuts! But he said, not too eagerly, "I guess maybe I
can. I walk here every day anyway. I don't have anything else I
have to do. I'll say hello if you're here." With a concealed sigh of
relief I said out loud "I'll be here," and inwardly, "Thanks for
answering the voice mail!" I was fairly confident that if John knew
someone was waiting for him, depending on him for something, he
would not take his life that night.

The next afternoon I set up camp in the same spot, with chair,
blanket, and book, but minus the nacho cheese flavored corn chips.
I waited for John. The afternoon wore on and there was no sign of
him. Nervously I told myself that I should have intervened more
aggressively the previous day. There was nothing I could do but
wait a little longer—and hope. I spent the time trying to read and
to enjoy the last of the warmth of the sun. Just at the point when I
had decided that he was not coming by, I looked up and saw him
in the distance, obviously looking for me. He had miscalculated
the place on the beach where I was. I waved; he turned, saw me,
and came trudging through the sand. We were both relieved to see
one another.

Wasting no words, John started the conversation, a little nervously. "So," he blurted out quickly, "you work in a medical school. With old people like me. Do you have any advice for me? I don't look forward to getting any older. It just doesn't seem worth the effort to get up in the morning anymore. You know, my wife died seventeen years ago. Just a few months after that I developed tinnitus in my good ear, and the ringing nearly drives me crazy. I hear sounds in my ear all the time. They tell me there's nothing they can do for it. I've come down here for eleven years every winter, and I live in a trailer court. It's nice. But it's too damn lonely. People are friendly enough, but they have their own lives.

"In the past I spent time with a nice lady who lives in the same court. But she's not here this year and no one answers her telephone in Michigan. I don't know what happened to her. I try to keep busy. I walk, bowl, do line dancing, play cards, a little golf. But its just passing the time. It's just too damn lonely! You must see plenty of people in the same boat. What do you tell them? I'd like to know if you have any advice at all! I don't think you can come up with much."

"I can think of two things you might try," I replied.

"Oh, yeah? What's that?"

"Eat broccoli and do volunteer work!"

"What?"

"Eat broccoli and do volunteer work—get involved in the lives of people who need you very much."

"But I already keep busy."

"It's not the same—keeping busy is focusing on you; doing volunteer work puts your attention on someone else. There's a very big difference." I proceeded to tell him that research indicates that volunteer work has positive effects on both the physical and mental health of the volunteer at all stages of the life span, not just in later life. In other words, volunteering is as good for all of us as oat bran!

"I used to do volunteer work—lots of it. One of my daughters taught handicapped children. I helped her with them. Then she got an administrative job and there was nothing for me to do. Anyway, it doesn't matter because every time I try to help someone, it backfires. I always get burned."

"Oh?"

"Always. I'm not going to do it anymore."

"What happened?"

"You say you want to put me in your book. Do you want to hear a real heart-throb?"

"Yes."

John proceeded to tell me his story—the immediate reason for his present distress. It seems that a number of years ago, after his mother died, he turned his portion of his inheritance, including the family homestead, over to his older sister and their younger, retarded sister. In addition, he persuaded all of his siblings to do the same, to enable the older daughter to take care of the younger one without having to worry about financial affairs. He let the family know that if anything happened to the older sister he would move a thousand miles back to Nova Scotia to take care of the disabled sister.

Three weeks before Christmas the caregiving sister suffered a series of strokes and was hospitalized; it became evident that she would no longer be able to live independently. Instead of informing John immediately, his daughter, who lived in the same town as her aunts and who wanted the house for herself, had both sisters placed in a nursing home and delayed calling John until all of the legal arrangements were made and the sisters were in their new living situation. Upon hearing what had happened John drove the thousand miles to Nova Scotia but was unable to change the course of events, because his daughter had been appointed the legal guardian of the sisters.

Distraught because of his sisters' situation and feeling incredibly betrayed by his favorite daughter, John left Nova Scotia, driving himself to his trailer in Nokomis. He was in such despair, so sad and angry, that he admitted that he had tried to drive off the road in an attempt to kill himself four times during that journey. He did not know why he had not carried through with the suicide. He felt he had nothing to live for; he had been betrayed by the one person he had never expected to abandon him.

He vowed that if he made it to Nokomis he would not do anything to help anyone ever again, for the rest of his life. The pain was just too great. Once in Florida, with no sign of his woman friend and no one to talk to, he started to seriously consider suicide again.

John ended his story and we just sat there in silence together for what seemed to be a long time. Then he said, "So what do say about that?"

I took a deep breath. My mind was a total blank. Help! "The only thing I know to say is to keep on helping; keep on reaching out."

"But why, if it backfires and I get burned?"

"Because the result really doesn't matter, even though we'd like to see successful results—we get lots of satisfaction from that. The important thing for our own well-being is that we continue, over and over again, to reach out and go beyond ourselves, our own narrowness, our own need to feel good about how helpful we are. I read something in a Jewish prayer book last September that had great meaning for me, and I memorized it. It said, 'I am the Lord. You think that I am far away from you, but in your love for your neighbor you will find Me; *not in his love for you but in your love for him*' (*Mahzor for Rosh Hashanah and Yom Kippur*). Anyway, we have no idea how the immediate result fits into the larger whole. Maybe your daughter needs this experience. I don't know."

"You mean my daughter might learn something from this? She knows how hurt I am, how disappointed I am in her. But she is young and she could change."

"Something like that. The real results may not even occur in your lifetime, though, so don't hold your breath waiting for her to apologize for messing everything up."

"What you're saying isn't easy to do. I don't know if I can be that unselfish. I don't know if I believe it all comes out in the wash. You're saying that it does."

"I don't know about that. I hope it does. I think I have faith that it does. The only thing I actually know, without a shadow of a doubt, is that if you continue to retreat into yourself, pulling away in anger and hurt from other people because you are angry with your daughter, you will end up losing your life, if not by suicide, then by illness—you will literally die of a broken heart—or some other vital organ. If you can, cling to the thought that the desire to help and the act of loving, of helping, is the most important part of all—that you'll find God in the process of loving. The successful, good results that you see and that come back to you are just frosting on the cake.

"There's a neat writer I'm reading now—here's the book, in fact. Anyway, her name is Julian of Norwich, and she lived in the fourteenth century in England as a kind of hermit. Julian had so much confidence in God that everything—even awful stuff—would ultimately be OK. Even when good efforts seemed to be turning out miserably. She's become famous for one saying: 'All shall be well, and all shall be well, and all manner of things shall be well.'

"Really, the only thing left for us to do after we've done our best is to let it all go and to trust in the goodness, the providence—actually, the creativity—of God."

"Well that certainly takes a load off the shoulders, but it doesn't sound like much fun," John said.

"That's probably because we're so darned success-oriented. We're afraid that others will judge us by how things turn out, the results of our efforts. And so we're afraid to try. We just need to relax, do what we can do, enjoy the process, and let God do whatever God wants to do."

All of a sudden I heard the message myself. What I was saying to John was what I needed so desperately to hear, too.

I realized, with deep grief and tremendous joy, why I had not been able to write, then revise, then release this book. All of my previous excuses for avoiding this task were true—to a degree. However, the bottom line, the real reason for my reluctance, was that I had not wanted to state publicly through my writing and in writing (which is more permanent and ultimately more public than speech) that what I am living for, who I am living for, and the reason why I am living, is Christ and his invitation to unity and the life of love.

All of my life I had been reluctant to claim this in front of certain people. I didn't want to be subjected to the ridicule of some of my peers. Had I been an ordained minister or an "official" church worker, the acceptability of the role itself might have protected me—I could have hidden behind the fact that I was speaking from my professional self, rather than from the deepest part of me. But as a lay woman whose official role is a researcher and clinician and teacher of geriatrics in a secular medical school, well, honestly, I was deeply embarrassed by what I had written. It did not fit the "image" I thought I had needed to create to protect myself from the judgment of my colleagues. This image was a major barrier to my relationship with God—a barrier which I had been denying and ignoring for a long time. It had to go. My refusal to write was nothing less than a denial of Christ and, at the same time, a denial of my truest self, my real identity.

We sat in silence for a long time, gazing beyond the beach to the sunset reflected on the calm water of the Gulf. Then John struggled up from the sand, brushed himself off and said, "All that and broccoli, too, huh?"

"Yup, I think so. Don't you like broccoli?"

"I'm like George Bush, but if it's that good for me I'll try it. I guess I could work with some retarded kids when I get back to Canada again, too."

He was on his legs and ready to go.

"By the way, Jane Marie" he said, speaking my name for the first time and looking at me with twinkling eyes and an ear-to-ear grin, "I'm a Mick (Irishman) and an R.C. Who are you?"

"I'm a Methodist and an R.C., too," I proudly proclaimed.

We laughed a final good-by.

And at some level we both realized that for a few hours, on a beach named for a life-nurturing grandmother, in the days of Epiphany, we had been more than strangers, more than any denominational label could describe or contain. We had lived together in the kingdom of God. I knew that I would carry this old man named John in my heart till the last of my earth-days, for we had been nothing less than Christ-gift to one another.

As I watched John walk away into the purple of the horizon I remembered another song and I sang its words—as my mother used to say—from "the cockles of my heart":

Lord, you have come to the seashore,
neither searching for the rich nor the wise,
desiring only that I should follow.

O Lord, with your eyes set upon me,
gently smiling,
you have spoken my name;
all I longed for
I have found by the water.
At your side, I will seek other shores.

I also realized for the very first time, as I watched John disappear, that old age is not only a "natural monastery"; for many people it is nothing less than a sharing in the Passion and Resurrection of Christ. Nothing less. We must honor and cherish, support and respect it as such.

REFERENCES

Coles, Robert. *The Spiritual Life of Children*. Boston: Houghton Mifflin Co., 1990.

Garrigou-Lagrange, Reginald. *The Three Ages of the Interior Life*. London: B. Herder Book Co., 1951.

Harper, Ralph. *On Presence: Variations and Reflections*. Philadelphia: Trinity Press International, 1991.

Jantzen, Grace. *Julian of Norwich: Mystic and Theologian*. New York: Paulist Press, 1988.

Kavanaugh, Kieran and Otilio Rodriguez. *The Collected Works of St. John of the Cross*. Washington, D.C.: ICS Publications, 1979.

Kelly, Thomas. *A Testament of Devotion*. San Francisco: HarperSanFrancisco, 1992.

Kinghorn, Kenneth. *Fresh Wind of the Spirit*. Grand Rapids: Francis Asbury Press, 1975.

Mahzor for Rosh Hashanah and Yom Kippur: A Prayer Book for The Days of Awe. New York: The Rabbinical Assembly.

Matthew the Poor. *The Communion of Love*. Crestwood, New York: St. Vladimir's Seminary Press, 1984.

May, Gerald. *The Awakened Heart*. San Francisco: HarperSanFrancisco, 1991.

Morse, Melvin and Paul Perry. *Closer to the Light*. New York: Villard Books, 1990.

Philipon, M.M. *Sister Elizabeth of the Trinity: Spiritual Writings*. Prepared for private circulation and distribution by Most Rev. Msgr. W. J. Doheny. C.S.C. Liverpool, 1962.

Rahner, Karl and Johann Metz. *The Courage to Pray*. New York: Crossroad Press, 1981.

Thibault, Jane Marie. "The Spiritual Call of Later Life" in *Weavings: A Journal of the Christian Spiritual Life*, Volume VI, Number 1, January/February 1991.

White, David, ed. *Eternal Quest: The Search for God*. Volume 1. New York: Paragon House, 1992.

Williams, Margery. *The Velveteen Rabbit*. Philadelphia: Running Press, 1981.

ABOUT THE AUTHOR

DR. JANE MARIE THIBAULT is Clinical Gerontologist and Assistant Professor of Family and Community Medicine at the School of Medicine at the University of Louisville in Kentucky. She holds the Ph.D. in Clinical Gerontology from the University of Chicago, the M.S.S.W. in Geriatric Social Work from the University of Louisville, the M.A. in Counseling Psychology from Chapman College in Orange, California, and the B.A. in English from Salve Regina University in Newport, Rhode Island.

Dr. Thibault's primary research is in the area of vocation and spiritual growth in later life. She is a contributing writer on issues of aging for numerous medical journals and for *Weavings: A Journal of the Christian Spiritual Life*. She is a highly sought lay preacher, workshop presenter, and retreat leader on issues of spirituality and aging. She is on the National Task Force for Spirituality and Aging for Catholic Charities, USA, and serves as a board member for the American Association of Homes and Services for the Aging.

With two colleagues, Dr. Thibault has designed a restraint-free chair for the frail elderly and is president of Eld-Arondak, Inc., the company that manufactures the chair.

She has developed a model for a contemplative community for older adults and works with a number of local congregations to develop spiritual companioning groups which enable elders to re-envision aging in the Christian context. Dr. Thibault considers herself an ecumenical Christian and holds membership in both The United Methodist Church and the Roman Catholic Church.

The author is married to Ronald Fryrear and lives in Louisville, Kentucky.